Ancient
Law of Kings

"Then Samuel told the people what the rights and duties of a king were. He wrote them down on a scroll and placed it before the LORD." *1 Samuel 10:25 NLT*

By Ken Johnson, Th.D.

Ancient Law of Kings
by Ken Johnson, Th.D.

Printed in the United States of America

ISBN – 10: 1719587345
ISBN – 13: 978-1719587341

Cover picture from the *Study of King David* by Julia Margaret Cameron, 1866

Unless otherwise indicated, Bible quotations are taken from the King James Version.

Contents

Introduction

The nation of Israel has returned to their land (AD 1948), taken back the Temple Mount (AD 1967), and won numerous wars. The preparation for the rebuilding of the temple has been ongoing, including the production of all necessary tools and the training of the Levitical priesthood. The Sanhedrin was revived (AD 2004) and practice sacrifices have begun (AD 2014). With all of this and the fact that the apostle Paul stated eventually all of Israel will be saved, we know more and more Jews will come to believe that Jesus (Yeshua) is truly the Messiah. As always, Satan will cast doubt and confusion into every person and group that he can. Recently we have seen much confusion about the Law and covenants by Christians, Messianic Jews, Noahides, and the several splinter groups of what is called the Hebrew Roots Movement. With differing ideas, they cannot all be correct. I believe what will bring cohesion to these groups, and eventually to all of Israel, is the understanding that Jesus (Yeshua) is the true Messiah and that our knowledge is darkened if we do not understand that the Mosaic Law is based on the Noahide Law of Genesis 9.

The concept of Noahide Law is this: God, through Noah, commanded all nations of the earth to observe seven moral laws. Each nation may add to them, but never change the original seven laws. One of these laws was to not commit blasphemy, but instead to listen to and follow the teachings of the prophets as much as Gentiles are allowed to. This succession of post-flood prophets started with Noah and his covenant recorded in Genesis 9. All nations were to wait for God to create a special nation (Israel) with special laws, ceremonies, and a priesthood. There would be more prophets, and eventually a Messiah, who would right all wrongs and reconcile us to God once and for all. This is taught in the Dead Sea Scrolls and in the Talmud, so it was the official doctrine of both the Pharisees and the Essenes. The ancient church fathers taught that the Messiah did come, and He created a new covenant for all. There were no longer Noahides nor Jews, each having to obey separate sets of laws written within the Old Testament Torah, but everyone could become a follower of the Messiah. They could become Christians or reject the Messiah and be damned. Christians would not keep the Jewish Sabbath, food laws, or ceremonies. In addition to the Dead Sea Scrolls, the Mishnah, and the Talmud, which was followed by the ancient Pharisees and Essenes, the modern day Orthodox Jews, Messianic Jews, and Christians believe in Noahide Law. Therefore, Jewish laws were never binding on Gentiles. The only group who does not believe this is the Hebrew Roots Movement. Some of the groups in the Hebrew Roots Movement reject the concept of Noahide Law. Instead, they believe that Noahide Law never existed, and that God gave the Mosaic Law not at Mount Sinai; but at Creation. God simply reaffirmed it through Moses. Therefore, they believe that all true believers, including Christians, must observe the Saturday Sabbath, eat only Kosher food, and keep the Jewish ceremonies the way the priests did. Let's be clear. Everyone today, except for some of the Hebrew Roots groups and some of the Sabbatarian cults, believes in Noahide Law. The most complete description of Noahide Law comes from the Law of Kings. This is why I published this book.

The Holy Spirit inspired Moses to write the Torah. These are the first five books of the Old Testament: Genesis, Exodus, Leviticus, Numbers, and Deuteronomy. Genesis is mainly history. The other four contain some history, and detail the Law that God gave to the nation of Israel through the angels and Moses.

To get a full understanding of the Law, we need to look closely to discover to whom the passage is speaking. If it is speaking about how "you" should do the temple sacrifices, then the "you" in that passage is referring to the Levitical priests and no one else. Only the Levites have permission to do temple sacrifices. If it says that Israel, along with the Gentiles who live in the land of Israel, must do or not do something, then everyone who lives in Israel is subject to those laws. If it is referring to how the kings of Israel or the Sanhedrin are to pass judgements, then those laws and responsibilities apply only to them. This can make proper understanding difficult unless the books of the Law are carefully studied. This was the situation when the prophet Samuel explained the laws and duties of what a king of Israel can and cannot do to the people. So, Samuel copied the Torah laws that apply *only* to the king and wrote them down in a scroll.

> "Samuel explained to the people the regulations concerning kingship. He wrote them in a scroll and placed it in the LORD's presence…"
> *1 Samuel 10:25 ISV*

This scroll is known as the *Law of Kings*. After Rome dispersed the Jews from the land of Israel, most of the oral law, traditions, and history were written down and codified in what is called the Mishnah. The Mishnah was completed about AD 200. In the twelfth century, Rabbi Maimonides wrote the *Mishneh Torah,* which is the Mishnah with Old Testament Scripture added. The *Law of Kings* is preserved in Rambam's *Mishneh Torah.*

Ancient Scrolls Verify Noahide Law

I believe it has been added to over the centuries; but the basic understanding of the Noahide laws is intact since other ancient texts corroborate them. The *Ancient Seder Olam 5* (AD 169) gives a detailed explanation of the Seven Noahide Laws. The *Ancient Book of Gad the Seer 9* (1000 BC) mentions that those who are forbidden to convert to Judaism must remain Noahides until the coming of Messiah.

Ancient Church Fathers Verify Noahide Law

Some of the ancient church fathers acknowledged that Noahide Law and the Melchizedekian priesthood existed before the Law of Moses was given on Mount Sinai.

> "[Adam] teaching them by what deeds of men the one God and Lord of all is pleased; and having exhibited to them the things that are pleasing to Him, appointed a perpetual law to all, which neither can be abrogated by enemies, nor is vitiated by any impious one, nor is concealed in any place, but which can be read by all. To them, therefore, by obedience to the law, all things were in abundance." *Clementine Homily 8.10*

> "In short, before the Law of Moses, written in stone-tables, I contend that there was a law unwritten, which was habitually understood naturally, and by the fathers was habitually kept. For whence was Noah 'found righteous,' if in his case the righteousness of a natural law had not preceded? Whence was Abraham accounted 'a friend of God,' if not on the ground of equity and righteousness, (in the observance) of a natural law? Whence was Melchizedek named 'priest of the most high God,' if, before the priesthood of the Levitical law, there were not Levites who were wont to offer sacrifices to God?" Tertullian, *Jews 2*

Dead Sea Scrolls Verify Noahide Law

The Dead Sea Scrolls mention some of the same information found in the *Law of Kings*. For instance, in the *Damascus Document 9* it directly mentions the "Law of the Gentiles." Gentile law, known as Noahide law, is taught in depth in *Law of Kings*, chapters 8-10. The *Temple Scroll*

48 mentions the laws regarding selling meat to Gentiles. *Temple Scroll 56* mentions the kings of Israel writing their own two Torah scrolls. *Temple Scroll 62* describes the official "offers of peace" that Joshua gave to the Canaanite nations occupying the land of Israel.

The Mishnah Torah

The Mishnah is divided into 14 sections:

1. HaMadda (Knowledge)
2. Ahavah (Love)
3. Zemanim (Times)
4. Nashim (Women)
5. Kedushah (Holiness)
6. Hafla'ah (Separation)
7. Zera'im (Seeds)
8. Avodah (Temple Service)
9. Korbanot (Offerings)
10. Sefer Taharah (Book of Purity)
11. Sefer Nezikim (Criminal and Tort Law)
12. Sefer Kinyan (Law of Marketplace)
13. Sefer Mishpatim (Civil Rights Law)
14. Sefer Shofatim (Laws of Legislators)

The fourteenth book, Sefer Shofatim, is divided into five sections.

1. Hilchot Sanhedrin
2. Hilchot 'Edut
3. Hilchot Mamrim

4. Hilchot Evel
5. Hilchot Melachim uMilhamoteyhem

We will concentrate on Hilchot Melachim uMilhamoteyhem which translates into the "Laws of the Kings and Wars." It is a valuable study for us today as it includes sections on Noahide Law, as well as the changes King Messiah will make when He sets up His kingdom. This shows us that Noahide Law is very real and very ancient. We will learn how the ancients viewed King Messiah.

Later Additions to This Text

If this is the *Laws of the Kings and Their Wars* written by the prophet Samuel, everything in it should align with the Scripture of his time. If a section of a chapter contains a quote from a Bible book that did not exist during the lifetime of the prophet Samuel, or an explanation from the "sages," we deem it to have been tampered with, or added to, by later Jewish editors who rejected the Messiah. Using these criteria, we will show that the sections 3.7b; 5.7-12; 7.15; 8.4-5; 10.8; 10.9a-b; 11.1-4; and 12.1-5 are additions to the original work. We will provide commentary in each section to prove this. This will allow us to see the original book of the *Law of Kings*.

Translation of the Law of Kings

1. Qualifications of Kings

1.1 Israel's Three Commands

God ordered Israel to fulfill these three commands when they entered the Promised Land:

1. Appoint a king that God chooses
2. Wipe out all traces of Amalek
3. Build God's house in His chosen place.

> "Thou shalt in any wise set *him* king over thee, whom the LORD thy God shall choose: *one* from among thy brethren shalt thou set king over thee: thou mayest not set a stranger over thee, which *is* not thy brother." *Deuteronomy 17:15*

> "Therefore it shall be, when the LORD thy God hath given thee rest from all thine enemies round about, in the land which the LORD thy God giveth thee *for* an inheritance to possess it, *that* thou shalt blot out the remembrance of Amalek from under heaven; thou shalt not forget *it*."
> *Deuteronomy 25:19*

> "But unto the place which the LORD your God shall choose out of all your tribes to put His name there, *even* unto His habitation shall ye seek, and thither thou shalt come:" *Deuteronomy 12:5*

1.2 The Order of the Three Commands

The three commands should be carried out in this order:

1. Appoint a king
2. Go to war with Amalek
3. Construct the temple.

> "Samuel also said unto Saul, The LORD sent me to anoint thee *to* be king over His people, over Israel: now therefore hearken thou unto the voice of the words of the LORD. Thus saith the LORD of hosts, I remember *that* which Amalek did to Israel, how he laid *wait* for him in the way, when he came up from Egypt. Now go and smite Amalek, and utterly destroy all that they have, and spare them not; but slay both man and woman, infant and suckling, ox and sheep, camel and ass." *1 Samuel 15:1-3*

> "And it came to pass, when the king sat in his house, and the LORD had given him rest round about from all his enemies; That the king said unto Nathan the prophet, See now, I dwell in an house of cedar, but the ark of God dwelleth within curtains." *2 Samuel 7:1-2*

If God commanded Israel to appoint a king, then why was God angry when the people asked Samuel for a king? Because it was not a request but a complaint. They were not trying to fulfill the command of God; but were rejecting Samuel's rule over them (which God had appointed).

> "And the LORD said unto Samuel, Hearken unto the voice of the people in all that they say unto thee: for they have not rejected thee, but they have rejected Me, that I should not reign over them."
> *1 Samuel 8:7*

1.3 Sanhedrin and Prophet Appoint Kings

Initially the king was to be appointed by the Sanhedrin (supreme court of Israel consisting of seventy elders), and a prophet of God. Joshua was appointed by the prophet Moses and his court and Saul and David were appointed by the prophet Samuel of Ramah and his court. This is still the preferred method of appointing a king.

1.4 King Must Be Native Born

Only a native-born Israelite (not a Gentile who converted to Judaism or a Noahide) should be made a king of Israel. A king must have at least a native-born mother or father. It does not matter if his ancestors were proselytes for generations.

> "Thou shalt in any wise set *him* king over thee, whom the LORD thy God shall choose: *one* from among thy brethren shalt thou set king over thee: thou mayest not set a stranger over thee, which is not thy brother." *Deuteronomy 17:15*

This applies to all positions of authority in Israel, not just the monarchy. A non-native-born Israelite shall not serve as an army commander, a leader of fifty, a leader of ten, or even be a public waterworks supervisor.

A judge or head of a family shall only be a native-born Israelite. When the Scripture says "from among your brethren," it implies *all* appointments are to be from "your brethren."

Commentary on 1.4
Noahides are defined in 8.10-11, and in 9 and 10.

1.5 King Must Be a Man

A woman shall not be appointed as king. The Torah always describes the monarchy in masculine terms. This also applies to all other forms of authority in Israel. Only men are to be appointed to any position of authority.

1.6 King Must Not Have Been a Servant

Neither butchers, barbers, bath-attendants, nor tanners shall be appointed king or High Priest. A man's profession does not make him unclean; but these professions are less prestigious than others, and people will not take these men seriously. Anyone who has been in one of these professions for even a single day, is disqualified for the monarchy.

1.7 Anointed with Special Oil

When a king is appointed, he is anointed with a special anointing oil reserved for this purpose.

> "And Samuel took a vial of oil and poured on his head, and kissed him, and said, Is it not because Jehovah has anointed you for a leader over His inheritance?" *1 Samuel 10:1 MKJV*

Once a king is anointed, he and his descendants are granted the monarchy eternally, because the monarchy is passed down by inheritance,

> "to the end that he may prolong *his* days in his kingdom, he, and his children, in the midst of Israel." *Deuteronomy 17:20b*

If the king dies leaving only a young son, the monarchy should be held for him until he matures, like Jehoiada did with Joash. The order of inheritance for the monarchy is the same as inheriting property. The older son is given precedence over the younger one.

Like the monarchy, all other positions of authority and appointments in Israel are transferred to one's children and grandchildren as inheritances eternally.

The above applies only if the son has the knowledge and the fear of God like that of his ancestors. If he has a fear of God like theirs, but does not have a knowledge like theirs, he shall be granted his father's crown and given instruction. However, even if he has an extensive knowledge of God, under no circumstances shall he who lacks the fear of God be appointed to any position of authority in Israel.

Once David was anointed king, the kingship belonged to him and to his male descendants forever.

> "And thine house and thy kingdom shall be established for ever before thee: thy throne shall be established forever." *2 Samuel 7:16*

David's "eternal throne" is conditional; it only applies to the righteous among his descendants,

> "If thy children will keep My covenant and My testimony that I shall teach them, their children shall also sit upon thy throne for evermore." *Psalms 132:12*

Despite this condition, God assured David that the monarchy would never be taken from his descendants eternally.

> "If they break My statutes and keep not My commandments, Then will I visit their transgression with the rod, and their iniquity with stripes. Nevertheless, My lovingkindness will I not utterly take from him, nor suffer My faithfulness to fail. My covenant will I not break, nor alter the thing that is gone out of My lips. Once have I sworn by My holiness that I will not lie unto David. His seed shall endure forever, and his throne as the sun before Me." *Psalms 89:31-36*

1.8 A Non-Davidic King

If a prophet appoints a king from any other tribe of Israel and that king follows the path of Torah, the commandments, and fights the wars of God, he is to be considered a true king, and all the regulations associated with the monarchy apply to him.

Even though the kingship was primarily given to David and his descendants, others can be allowed to rule as king. For example, Ahijah the Shilonite appointed Jeroboam and told him:

> "And it shall be, if thou wilt hearken unto all that I command thee, and wilt walk in My ways, and do *that is* right in My sight, to keep My statutes and My commandments, as David My servant did; that I will be with thee, and build thee a sure house, as I built for David, and will give Israel unto thee."
> *1 Kings 11:38*

Similarly, Ahijah told him:

> "And unto his son will I give one tribe, that David My servant may have a light alway before Me in Jerusalem, the city which I have chosen Me to put My name there." *1 Kings 11:36*

1.9 The Davidic Dynasty

The kings of the Davidic dynasty will prevail eternally.

> "And thine house and thy kingdom shall be established for ever before thee: thy throne shall be established forever." *2 Samuel 7:16*

In contrast, should a king arise from other Israelites, their monarchy will eventually come to an end. For behold, Jeroboam was told:

> "And I will for this afflict the seed of David, but not for ever." *1 Kings 11:39*

1.10 Anointing Oils

Kings of Israel are not anointed with the special anointing oil, but with Afarsimon oil. Only a descendent of David may be appointed as king in Jerusalem and anointed with the special anointing oil.

1.11 Anointing Near a Spring

A king of the Davidic dynasty should only be anointed near a spring.

1.12 Succession of Princes

A son who succeeds his father as king is not anointed unless he inherits the throne when there is a dispute over the inheritance or during a civil war. Under these circumstances, he should be anointed in order to remove all doubt to his authority.

They only anointed Solomon because of Adonijah's claim; Jehoash, because of Athaliah's rebellion; and Jehoahaz, because of Jehoiakim's dispute.

2. Duties to the King

2.1 Respect for the King
The king must be shone great honor. All men must have an attitude of awe and fear of him in their hearts. The command to "appoint a king" [Deuteronomy 17:15]: implies the obligation to show him proper respect.

No one shall ride on his horse, sit on his throne, use his scepter, wear his crown, or use any of his utensils. When he dies, they should all be burned before his bier.

Only another king is allowed to make use of his servants, maids, and attendants. This is why Abishag was permitted to Solomon, but prohibited to Adonijah.

2.2 King's Wife
However, a king's wife is forbidden to ever be intimate with another person. Even another king may not marry a king's widow or his divorced ex-wife.

2.3 King's Privacy
It is forbidden to watch the king while he is naked, having his hair cut, in the baths, or is drying himself afterwards.

The king is forbidden to perform the ritual of *chalitzah* because, it is disrespectful to spit on the king.

> "then his brother's widow is to come to him in the sight of the elders, pull his sandal off his foot, spit in his face, and reply, 'So will it be done to the man who does not build up his brother's house.'" *Deuteronomy 25:9*

Even if the king wants to perform this command / ritual and is willing to undergo the disrespect, he is forbidden to do so because a king's honor must be preserved.

Since he is forbidden perform *chalitzah*, this makes him ineligible to participate in *yibbum*. Since it is also forbidden to initiate *yibbum* with the king's wife, *chalitzah* is not performed for her either. Instead, she must remain in her state of attachment eternally.

Commentary on 2.3
Yibbum is raising up seed for a deceased brother. Chalitzah is a ritual refusing to enter into a Yibbum. The scribes are interpreting "her attachment" to mean that she must remain single and celibate; but I believe this means that if she remarries, her child cannot be heir to the throne.

2.4 King in Mourning

The king is not to leave his palace for a relative's funeral. He should sit on a low couch to show mourning and any before him should sit on the ground.

When he enters the temple courtyard, if he is of David's descendants, he may sit, for the kings of the Davidic dynasty are the only ones who may sit in the temple courtyard.

> "Then went King David in, and sat before the LORD, and he said, Who *am* I, O Lord GOD? and what *is* my house, that thou hast brought me hitherto?" *2 Samuel 7:18*

2.5 Showing Proper Respect / Prostration

A king should have his hair cut daily. He should dress and adorn himself in fine clothing,

> "Thine eyes shall see the king in his beauty…" *Isaiah 33:17a*

He is to sit on his throne in his palace with his crown on his head.

When the king summons someone, they shall present themselves before him, standing first, then prostrating themselves on the ground. This includes prophets.

> "And they told the king, saying, Behold Nathan the prophet. And when he was come in before the king, he bowed himself before the king with his face to the ground." *1 Kings 1:23*

However, the High Priest only comes before the king if he desires to do so. The High Priest does not stand before the king; but rather the king stands before the High Priest!

> "And he shall stand before Eleazar the priest, who shall ask *counsel* for him after the judgment of Urim before the LORD: at his word shall they go out, and at his word they shall come in, *both* he, and all the children of Israel with him, even all the congregation." *Numbers 27:21*

However, the High Priest should show the curtesy of honoring the king by having the king seated and standing in the king's presence when he visits. But the king must stand before the High Priest when he consults the Urim and Thumim.

Likewise, it is common curtesy for the king to honor Torah students when they have an audience. He should stand to welcome the Sanhedrin and the Sages of Israel and seat them at his side.

King Jehosephat of Judah followed this practice. Whenever any Torah scholar or one of their students would come to him, he would rise from his throne, kiss, and address him as "My teacher and master."

This only applies when the king is alone in his palace. When in private, only his servants with him, he should act in this way. However, he should not act this way before the people in public. He should not stand before anyone, nor speak gently with them. He should address a person only using his proper name in order that the people will fear and respect him.

2.6 King Must Be Humble

Even though the Torah grants him great honor, and everyone is obligated to revere him, he is commanded to be lowly and humble at heart.

> "For I *am* poor and needy, and my heart is wounded within me." *Psalms 109:22*

Nor should he be exceedingly prideful over Israel.

> "That his heart be not lifted up above his brethren, and that he turn not aside from the commandment, *to* the right hand, or *to* the left:"
> *Deuteronomy 17:20a*

He shall seek the welfare of both the small and the great, showing grace and mercy to all. He shall protect the honor even of the lowliest man.

When he speaks to the people as a community, he should speak with gentleness,

> "Then David the king stood up upon his feet, and said, Hear me, my brethren, and my people: *As for me*, I *had* in mine heart to build an house of rest for the ark of the covenant of the LORD, and for the footstool of our God, and had made ready for the building:" *1 Chronicles 28:2*

Similarly,

> "If thou wilt be a servant unto this people this day, and wilt serve them, and answer them, and speak good words to them, then they will be thy servants forever." *1 Kings 12:7b*

He should always show great humility. No one is greater than Moses, our teacher, but he said,

> "And Moses said, …what *are* we? your murmurings *are* not against us, but against the LORD." *Exodus 16:8*

Just as a nurse cares for the need of an infant so the king must bear the difficulties, burdens, complaints, and anger of the nation.

> "He chose David also, His servant, and took him from the sheepfolds: From following the ewes great with young He brought him to feed Jacob His people, and Israel His inheritance. So he fed them according to the integrity of his heart; and guided them by the skillfulness of his hands."
> *Psalms 78:70-72*

The prophets describe a shepherd's behavior as:

> "He shall feed his flock like a shepherd: he shall gather the lambs with his arm, and carry *them* in his bosom, *and* shall gently lead those that are with young." *Isaiah 40:11*

3. Requirements of the King

3.1 King's Own Torah Scroll

During a king's reign, he must write his own Torah scroll in addition to the scroll his ancestors left him. The Sanhedrin (a court of seventy-one elders) should check his scroll's accuracy by comparing it to the Torah scroll kept in the temple courtyard.

The king must write two Torah scrolls if his ancestors did not leave him a Torah scroll or that scroll was lost.

The first one he is obligated to write, as is every individual Israelite, and place in his treasury.

The second, he should have with him at all times except when he enters a place where it is not fit to read the words of Torah (e.g. a lavatory or bath).

This scroll should be with him when he goes to and returns from war, and when he sits in judgment. It should be placed across from him when he dines.

> "It will remain with him, and he will read in it all the days of his life, in order to learn to fear Adonai his God and keep all the words of this Torah and these statutes." *Deuteronomy 17:19 TLV*

Commentary on 3.1
The king writes one Torah scroll to teach his children, as all Israelites must do, and a second one for his use on a daily basis. The first might be a full Torah and the second might be this *Law of Kings*.

3.2 King Has Eighteen Wives Maximum

The oral tradition teaches that he may take no more than eighteen wives (this includes concubines). He may divorce one of his wives and replace her by marrying another. If he takes an additional wife and has relations with her, he shall be lashed.

> "Nor should he multiply wives for himself, so that his heart does not turn aside, nor multiply much silver and gold for himself." *Deuteronomy 17:17*

3.3 King's Amount of Horses

He may only take the amount of horses he needs for himself and his cavalry. It is even forbidden for him to have one additional horse to run before him, as is the custom of other kings. If he adds an additional horse, he shall be lashed.

3.4 King's Collection of Gold and Silver

He may collect only as much silver and gold as he needs to pay for his soldiers, servants, and attendants. He shall not hoard gold and silver in his personal treasury. This would cause him to glorify himself through pride.

Any excess of gold and silver he accumulates should be placed in the temple treasury for the future needs of the people, and for possible wars. It is a duty to accumulate wealth for the temple treasury. He is to be lashed if he amasses excessive personal wealth in his own treasury.

> "Nor should he multiply wives for himself, so that his heart does not turn aside, nor multiply much silver and gold for himself." *Deuteronomy 17:17*

3.5 The King and Wine

The king is forbidden to drink wine to the point of intoxication.

> "*It is* not for kings, O Lemuel, *it is* not for kings to drink wine, or for rulers to crave strong drink."
> *Proverbs 31:4*

Instead, he should study Torah and be involved with the needs of Israel day and night,

> "And it shall be with him, and he shall read therein all the days of his life: that he may learn to fear the LORD his God, to keep all the words of this law and these statutes, to do them."
> *Deuteronomy 17:19*

3.6 King is Not to Be Influenced by His Wives

The king should not be too focused on his relationships with his wives. Even if he has only one wife, he should not constantly have her with him. This is the practice of fools.

> "Give not thy strength unto women, nor thy ways to that which destroyeth kings." *Proverbs 31:3*

Torah forbids a king from taking many wives because his heart may go astray,

> "Nor shall he multiply wives to himself, so that his heart does not turn away…"
> *Deuteronomy 17:17 MKJV*

The king must be more dedicated to Torah than others because he guides the nation of Israel.

> "all the days of his life." *Deuteronomy 17:19*

3.7 Davidic Kings May Testify

The kings of the Davidic dynasty may both testify and be judged. [The sages decreed that other kings of Israel cannot testify or be judged. They may not testify, nor be accused. In their arrogance they may cause a tragedy or lose faith.]

Commentary on 3.7
The sages comment [in brackets] was added later because they knew of the kings' arrogance by experience. This is not part of the original Law.

3.8 King May Execute Rebels

The king may execute anyone who rebels against him. This includes anyone who defies the king when he is banished or placed under house arrest. The king may execute him if he desires.

> "Whosoever *he be* that doth rebel against thy commandment, and will not hearken unto thy words in all that thou commandest him, he shall be put to death:" *Joshua 1:18*

Likewise, the king may execute anyone who embarrasses or shames him as Shimei son of Gera did David.

The king may punish with imprisonment anyone who dishonors him, or he may have them beaten. He may execute only by decapitation. However, he is forbidden to merely confiscate their property, because that is theft.

Commentary on 3.8
The event of Shimei son of Gera is recorded in 1 Kings 2:8-9.

3.9 God's Commands Outrank the King's

A person who refuses a king's command because he is observing even a minor command of the LORD, is not liable. The Laws of God have precedence over the king's commands. Also, if a king decrees to alter a command of Yahweh, his decree is to be ignored.

3.10 King's Discretion in Execution

The king has the authority to execute an accused murderer even if:

1. evidence is inconclusive
2. he was not warned before he killed the victim
3. there is only one witness

4. it seems like an accidental killing.

He may execute several in a single day, and publicly hang their corpses for several days in order to cast fear into the hearts of the wicked and destroy their power in the land.

Commentary on 3.10
Point 2 is referring to someone suspected of using self-defense as an excuse to murder. See 9.4

4. Powers of the King

4.1 Taxation

The king may levy taxes upon the people of Israel for his needs or for war. He may also create a sales tax. It is forbidden to avoid paying these taxes. The king has the right to seize the property or execute anyone who does not pay these taxes.

> "He will take the tenth of your sheep: and ye shall be his servants." *1 Samuel 8:17*

> "...all the people *that is* found therein shall be tributaries unto thee, and they shall serve thee." *Deuteronomy 20:11*

From these verses, it is clear that the king may create taxes and fix a sales tax. The law clearly states that the king is entitled to create statutes regarding all matters related to taxes.

4.2 The King May Draft Men

The king may also draft valiant men and men of war throughout Israel to be employed as soldiers for his chariots and cavalry.

He may also appoint them as his servants, attendants, body guards, and footmen to run before him.

> "And he said, This will be the manner of the king that shall reign over you: He will take your sons, and appoint *them* for himself, for his chariots, and *to be* his horsemen; and *some* shall run before his chariots." *1 Samuel 8:11*

4.3 Conscription of Craftsmen

Similarly, he may conscript those necessary for him from the nation's craftsmen. He must pay their wages. He may also take all the beasts, servants, and maids that are necessary for his tasks. He must pay their hire or their value.

> "And he will take your menservants, and your maidservants, and your goodliest young men, and your asses, and put *them* to his work."
> *1 Samuel 8:16*

4.4 Wives and Concubines

The king may take his wives and concubines from any territory of Israel. "Wives" are women whom he marries (gives a *ketubah* and *kiddushin*). Concubines are women who are not given a *ketubah* and *kiddushin*. If the king has performed the act of *yichud*, that alone means he acquires the woman and may have relations with her.

Commoners are forbidden to have concubines. The only similar relationship is the union with a Hebrew maid servant after she has been designated by her master.

The king may use his palace concubines as cooks, bakers, and perfumers,

> "And he will take your daughters to be confectionaries, and to be cooks, and to be bakers."
> *1 Samuel 8:13*

Commentary on 4.4

A *ketubah* is a wedding contract.

A *kiddushin* is a wedding ceremony entitling a woman to compensation if divorced.

Yichud is being alone with a woman in a secluded place.

A maidservant is only similar to a concubine in the sense that the maidservant already resides in the home of the one who betrothed her, and she has not yet received a Ketubah (marriage contract) from her master or his son. See Exodus 21:7-11.

4.5 Appointment of Leaders

The king may force those who are fit to serve to be officers, leaders of thousands, and leaders of fifties.

> "And he will appoint him captains over thousands, and captains over fifties;"
> *1 Samuel 8:12*

4.6 Demand for Support of Troops

The king may take fields, olive groves, and vineyards for his servants during a war. These places may be commandeered if needed to support the troops. He must pay for what is taken.

> "And he will take your fields, and your vineyards, and your oliveyards, *even* the best *of them*, and give *them* to his servants." *1 Samuel 8:14*

4.7 King May Take a Tenth Tax

The king may take a tenth of the produce of the seed, the orchards, and the newborn beasts.

> "He will take the ten-percent tax of your flocks, and you will become his servants."
> *1 Samuel 8:17 CJB*

4.8 King Messiah's Land Portion

King Messiah may take a thirteenth portion of the land of Israel for His own. This will be an eternal allotment for Him.

> **Commentary on 4.8**
> The thirteenth portion is referred to in Ezekiel 45:7-8; 48:21-22. Notice the Messiah is eternal.

4.9 Property Returned to the King

The property of all those executed by the king reverts to the king. The king also obtains all the treasures and property belonging to the kings of the kingdoms which he conquers.

Soldiers may take any other spoil. They must bring it to the king, who is entitled to one half of the spoil. He takes his portion first. The second half of the spoil is then divided between the combat soldiers and the people who remained behind to guard the camp. It is divided equally among them.

> "For as the portion of him who goes down to battle, so shall be his share who remains by the baggage. They shall share together."
> *1 Samuel 30:24 LITV*

4.10 Lands Conquered By the King

The king takes possession of all lands that he conquers. He portions out parcels of land to his servants and soldiers as he sees fit and keeps the rest for himself. The king has sole discretion in these matters.

The purpose and intent for everything he does should be to spread the true faith, fill the world with justice, and destroy the power of the wicked by waging the wars of God. For this is the king's entire purpose.

> "…that our king may judge us, and go out before us, and fight our battles." *1 Samuel 8:20*

5. King's Wartime Powers

5.1 War by Commandment

A king should not wage other wars before a War by Commandment. A "War by Commandment" is defined as:

1. War against the seven Canaanite nations
2. War against Amalek
3. War against an enemy who attacks Israel.

Only after the Wars by Commandment are fought, may the king wage an Authorized War. An "Authorized War" is defined as "a war fought with other nations to expand Israel's borders, greatness, or reputation."

> **Commentary on 5.1**
> All nations should look to Israel for guidance and protection.

5.2 Authorized War - Sanhedrin's Permission

Permission of the court is not needed to wage a War by Commandment. Rather, the king may go out under his own volition with his troops. In contrast, he may not enter into an Authorized War unless approved by the Sanhedrin (court of seventy-one judges).

5.3 Wartime Damages

The king may trample over fences, surrounding fields, or vineyards to make his way to a war. No one can take issue with this. There are no exceptions and no limit to the way the king may take. He does not need to go around an individual's vineyard or field. Instead, he should proceed straight to the warfront.

5.4a Annihilate the Canaanite Nations

It is a positive commandment to annihilate the seven nations that dwelled in the land of Israel.

> "But thou shalt utterly destroy them; *namely*, the Hittites, and the Amorites, the Canaanites, and the Perizzites, the Hivites, and the Jebusites; as the LORD thy God hath commanded thee:"
> *Deuteronomy 20:17*

5.4b Annihilate All Canaanite Pagans

Whoever stumbles upon one of them and does not kill them violates a negative commandment. Their memory is to be obliterated.

> "But of the cities of these people, which the LORD thy God doth give thee *for* an inheritance, thou shalt save alive nothing that breatheth:"
> *Deuteronomy 20:16*

5.5a Destroy All Traces of Amalek

It is a positive commandment to destroy the memory of Amalek.

> "...Thou shalt blot out the remembrance of Amalek from under heaven; thou shalt not forget *it.*" *Deuteronomy 25:19*

5.5b Teach Future Generations about Amalek

Also, it is a positive commandment to constantly remember Amalek's ambush of Israel and other evil deeds to arouse our hatred of them. It is forbidden to forget our hatred and enmity for them.

> "Remember what Amalek did unto thee by the way, when ye were come forth out of Egypt;" *Deuteronomy 25:17*

Commentary on 5.5b

If you do not remember them and their treachery, you will not recognize others when they betray you. e.g. Nazi Germany.

5.6 Conquered Lands

All the lands Israel conquers in wars, when led by a duly-appointed king and approved by the court, are considered as conquered by the Israeli people. Thus, those lands have the exact same status as the land of Israel conquered by Joshua. This only applies if they were conquered after the Wars by Commandment as described in the Torah.

5b. Lands of Israel and Egypt (Sage's Additions)

Commentary on 5b
This second part of chapter 5 (Sections 7-12) gives multiple proofs that they have been added centuries later by sages and are not a part of the original text. (See the introductory chapter of this book for details.) Therefore, I have separated them into a chapter of their own, 5b.

5.7 Land of Egypt Forbidden

It is forbidden to dwell anywhere in the land of Egypt. Any other land is acceptable. The forbidden territory is four hundred parsah square that borders on the Mediterranean Sea, the Arabian desert, and Sudan. This prohibition includes Alexandria.

The Torah warns in three places not to return to Egypt:

1. Exodus 14:13 says, "You shall see them again no more forever."
2. Deuteronomy 17:16 says, "God has told you, you must never again return on that path."
3. Deuteronomy 28:68, says "You shall not see it again."

Commentary on 5.7
The three Scriptures are given out of context.

In the first text, Moses told the Israelites they would never see their Egyptian captors again. (The Egyptian army died in the Red Sea.)

> "And Moses said unto the people, Fear ye not, stand still, and see the salvation of the LORD, which he will shew to you today: for the Egyptians whom ye have seen today, ye shall see them again no more forever."
> *Exodus 14:13*

In the second text, God orders Israel not go to Egypt to buy horses.

> "But he shall not multiply horses to himself, nor cause the people to return to Egypt, to the end that he should multiply horses: forasmuch as the LORD hath said unto you, Ye shall henceforth return no more that way."
> *Deuteronomy 17:16*

The third text is a prophecy that they *will* go back to Egypt.

> "And the LORD shall bring thee into Egypt again with ships, by the way whereof I spake unto thee, Thou shalt see it no more again: and there ye shall be sold unto your enemies for bondmen and bondwomen, and no man shall buy *you.*" *Deuteronomy 28:68*

This may have been added based on the prophecy of a future time when Egypt would be uninhabitable (Ezekiel 29:12-13).

5.8 Egypt and Trade

It is permitted to return to Egypt for business purposes. A king may pass through Egypt to attack another nation. An Israeli is only forbidden to settle there.

There is no punishment (lashes or otherwise) for breaking this law, because once one enters Egypt, he is outside of our jurisdiction; and should he decide to settle there, no Israeli land deed would be involved.

> "After the doings of the land of Egypt, wherein ye dwelt, shall ye not do: and after the doings of the land of Canaan, whither I bring you, shall ye not do: neither shall ye walk in their ordinances."
> *Leviticus 18:3*

Commentary on 5.8
This contradicts 5.6 which states any land Israel acquires belongs to the people of Israel; so naturally they could settle in any part of Egypt taken in battle.

5.9 The Return to Israel

It is forbidden to leave the land of Israel for the Diaspora at any time except:

1. to study Torah
2. to marry
3. to prevent Gentiles from taking one's property.

Once these are accomplished, one must return to the land of Israel.

One may also leave the land of Israel to conduct business. It is only forbidden to leave with the intent of permanently settling in the Diaspora, unless the famine in the land of Israel is so severe that wheat is sold for double the normal price.

This applies when one cannot afford to buy food, it is either too expensive, or one cannot find work.

Even though he would be permitted to leave the land of Israel under these circumstances, it is not pious behavior. Mahlon and Chilion were two great men of their generation. They left the land of Israel only out of great famine. Nevertheless, God found them worthy of death.

Commentary on 5.9
Abraham, Isaac, and Jacob all left the land at times due to famines. Anyone else would also. Mahlon's and Chilion's deaths had nothing to do with leaving Israel in a time of famine. Their father took them. See Ruth 1:2-5

5.10 Kissing the Land of Israel

When great sages came to Israel, they would kiss the borders of the land of Israel, kiss its stones, and roll in its dust, based on Psalm 102.

> "For Your servants take pleasure in her stones, And show favor to her dust."
> *Psalms 102:14 NKJV*

Commentary on 5.10
Some rabbis who migrate to Israel actually do this. This passage must be where they get the idea. That does not mean that they should. It borders on making the land of Israel an idol.

5.11 Sages' Concept of Land Atonement

The sages commented: "Whoever dwells in the land of Israel will have his sins forgiven" based on:

Ancient Law of Kings

> "And the inhabitant shall not say, I am sick: the people that dwell therein *shall be* forgiven *their* iniquity." *Isaiah 33:24*

Even if one only walks four cubits in the land of Israel, he will merit the world to come. The one who is buried in Israel receives the same atonement as if the place in which he is buried is an altar of atonement,

> "His land will atone for His people."
> *Deuteronomy 32:43 (Badly Paraphrased)*

In contrast, the prophet Amos (7:17) used the expression, 'You shall die in an impure land' as a prophecy of divine judgment.

There cannot be any comparison between the merit of a person who lives in the land of Israel and one whose body is brought there just for burial. Still, great sages would bring their dead to Israel, for example, our patriarchs, Jacob, and Joseph the Righteous.

Commentary on 5.11

Now the sages are saying that they actually believe moving to the land of Israel and being buried there will atone for their sin and merit them eternal life. To gain eternal life, one must accept Jesus the Messiah as their Lord and Savior, not the land of Israel. The New Testament explains this clearly.

The Dead Sea Scrolls show that the patriarchs wanted their remains transferred to Israel, not to obtain a better resurrection, but as a testament to prophecy and a legacy to their descendants.

5.12 Leaving the Land of Israel

At all times, one should dwell in the land of Israel even in a primarily Gentile city, rather than dwell in the Diaspora, in a primarily Jewish city.

The sages said, "Whoever leaves land of Israel for the Diaspora is considered as if he worships idols."

> "...They have driven me out this day from abiding in the inheritance of the LORD, saying, Go, serve other gods." 1 *Samuel 26:19*

> "And Mine hand shall be upon the prophets that see vanity, and that divine lies: ...neither shall they enter into the land of Israel; and ye shall know that I am the Lord GOD." *Ezekiel 13:9*

Just as it is forbidden to leave the land of Israel for the Diaspora, it is also forbidden to leave Babylon for other lands,

> "They shall be carried to Babylon, and there shall they be until the day that I visit them, saith the LORD; then will I bring them up, and restore them to this place." *Jeremiah 27:22*

Commentary on 5.12

God has called many to leave their lands and settle in new lands to spread the Gospel. This may be, in general, a good idea for a Jew; but it cannot be a law.

6. Offers of Peace

6.1a Offer of Noahide Peace

Neither a War by Commandment nor an Authorized War shall be waged against anyone before they are offered the opportunity of peace.

> "When you advance on a town to attack it, first offer it terms for peace." *Deuteronomy 20:10 CJB*

If the enemy city accepts the offer of peace and pledges to keep the seven Noahide Laws, none of them should be killed. Rather, they should be subjugated.

> "And it shall be, if it makes the answer of peace and opens to you, then all the people found in it shall be forced laborers to you, and they shall serve you." *Deuteronomy 20:11 MKJV*

6.1b Subjugation and Tribute

If they agree to pay tribute but refuse subjugation, or agree to subjugation but refuse to pay tribute, peace shall be denied. They must humbly accept both.

Subjugation:

1. They agree to judicially being on a lower level
2. They agree to never rebel against Israel
3. They agree to remain subjugated under Israeli law

4. They may never be appointed over a Jew in any matter.

Tribute: They must pledge to support the king's service with their money and with their persons; (e.g. building walls, strengthening fortresses, building the king's palace, and the like).

> "And this is the reason of the levy which king Solomon raised; for to build the house of the LORD, and his own house, and Millo, and the wall of Jerusalem… *And* all the people *that were* left of the Amorites, Hittites, Perizzites, Hivites, and Jebusites… upon those did Solomon levy a tribute of bondservice unto this day. But of the children of Israel did Solomon make no bondmen: but they *were* men of war, and his servants, and his princes, and his captains, and rulers of his chariots, and his horsemen." *1 Kings 9:15, 20-22*

Solomon took bondsmen from the Noahides. Only the children of Israel were appointed as his men of war, personal servants, princes, captains, officers, charioteers, and horsemen.

Commentary on 6.1
Under the subjugation law, they were free to leave the land of Israel to live the way they wished (in idolatry) or free to stay in the land of Israel and submit to Israeli / Noahide law.

6.2 Royal Discretion in Settlements

In any settlement offer, the king is entitled to take up to a maximum of one of these three options:

1. Half of their financial resources (50% tax)
2. All their land property (no movable property)
3. All their movable property (no land).

Commentary on 6.2
"Taking all of their land" means they are exiled (with all their belongings) to a land where they can live in idolatry. "Taking all of their personal property" means they are bondservants to the king (if they choose to stay), like the Gibeonites.

6.3 Lying About the Noahide Laws

It is forbidden to lie to Gentiles when making a peace covenant or to be untruthful to them after they have made peace and accepted the seven Noahide Laws.

6.4 Grounds for War

If Gentiles refuse the peaceful settlement, or if they agree to a peaceful settlement but refuse to accept the seven Noahide Laws, war should be waged against them.

All males past majority age should be killed. Their money and their children [minors] should be taken as spoil, but neither women nor children should be killed.

> "But the women, and the little ones, and the cattle, and all that is in the city, *even* all the spoil thereof, shalt thou take unto thyself; and thou shalt eat the

> spoil of thine enemies, which the LORD thy God hath given thee." *Deuteronomy 20:14*

The women-and-children clause applies only to an Authorized War fought with other nations. If any of the seven Canaanite nations or Amalek refuse to accept a peaceful settlement, not one soul of them shall be left alive [Because they are dwelling in the land of Israel].

> "Thus shalt thou do unto all the cities *which are* very far off from thee, which are not of the cities of these nations. But of the cities of these people, which the LORD thy God doth give thee *for* an inheritance, thou shalt save alive nothing that breatheth:" *Deuteronomy 20:15-16*

However, Amalek should be completely wiped out,

> "...thou shalt blot out the remembrance of Amalek from under heaven; thou shalt not forget it." *Deuteronomy 25:19*

We know offers of peace were made, but not accepted by; any of the Canaanite nations except the Hivites of Gibeon,

> "There was not a city that made peace with the children of Israel, save the Hivites the inhabitants of Gibeon: all *other* they took in battle. For it was of the LORD to harden their hearts, that they

> should come against Israel in battle, that He might destroy them utterly…" *Joshua 11:19-20*

6.5 Joshua's Letters of Peace

Before Israel entered the promised land, Joshua sent three letters to the Canaanite nations:

- First letter: "Whoever desires to flee, should flee"
- Second letter: "Whoever desires to accept a peaceful settlement, should make peace"
- Final letter: "'Whoever desires war, should do battle."

The Gibeonites deceived Israel because they received the first letter to the Canaanite nations but did not send a response. They did not understand the laws of Israel and thought they would not receive another offer of peace.

The princes of Israel wanted to slay the Gibeonites because they were deceived into making a covenant with them and it is forbidden to make a covenant with any nation inside of Israel. Instead, the Gibeonites should have been subjugated or left the land of Israel.

> "And when the LORD thy God shall deliver them before thee; thou shalt smite them, *and* utterly destroy them; thou shalt make no covenant with them, nor shew mercy unto them:"
> *Deuteronomy 7:2*

Since the Gibeonite oath was given to Israel under false pretenses, it would have been justifiable to kill them for the deception. They chose not to kill them because it might have caused dishonor to God's name.

6.6 Ammon and Moab

No offer of peaceful settlement should be made to Ammon and Moab,

> "Thou shalt not seek their peace nor their prosperity all thy days forever."
> *Deuteronomy 23:6*

But it is written:

> "He shall dwell with thee, *even* among you, in that place which he shall choose in one of thy gates, where it liketh him best: thou shalt not oppress him." *Deuteronomy 23:16*

Even though we cannot offer the *nations* of Ammon or Moab peaceful settlements, if an *individual* of Ammon or Moab sues for peace, we may accept their offer.

Commentary on 6.6
"Suing for peace" means coming before a Jewish court to declare themselves Noahides.

6.7 Besieging a City on Three Sides

When conquering a city, the besiegement should not surround it completely. Troops should only be on three of the four sides to make a way for the inhabitants to flee for their lives. According to tradition, the LORD commanded them to array the siege this way.

> “And they warred against the Midianites, as the LORD commanded Moses; and they slew all the males.” *Numbers 31:7*

6.8 Fruit Trees

Do not cut down fruit trees outside a city or prevent an irrigation ditch from watering them so that they dry up.

> “When thou shalt besiege a city a long time, in making war against it to take it, thou shalt not destroy the trees thereof by forcing an axe against them:” *Deuteronomy 20:19*

This applies to a siege and all other situations. Anyone who cuts down a fruit tree with a destructive intent, should be lashed. Torah only prohibits cutting down a tree with a destructive intent. A fruit tree may be cut down if:

1. It causes damage to other trees
2. It causes damage to fields belonging to others
3. A high price could be received for its wood.

6.9 Cutting Down Trees

Non-fruit bearing trees can be cut down even if there is no need to do so.

Fruit bearing trees may be cut down when they are old and bear little fruit which is not worth the effort required to take care of it.

An olive tree must make at least one-eighth of a pint (quarter of a kav) of olives and a date palm must make at least one-half pint (a kav) of dates to be worth the effort.

6.10 Do not Destroy

This prohibition does not apply only to trees. It applies to anyone who destroys utensils, garments, buildings, stops up a spring, or ruins food with a destructive intent.

6.11 Battle on a Sabbath

A siege against a Gentile city should start at least three days before a Sabbath. Battle may be waged every day, including Sabbaths. This applies to both Wars by Commandment and Authorized Wars.

> "When you shall lay siege to a city many days, to fight against it, to capture it…"
> *Deuteronomy 20:19 LITV*

6.12a Army Encampments

The army of Israel may encamp anywhere.

6.12b Wartime Burial

Anyone killed during a war should be buried where he falls.

6.13 The Four Leniencies

Four leniencies are permitted in an army camp:

1. One may eat the *Demai*. (Priestly part of the food)
2. One doesn't have to wash his hands before eating
3. Wood may be gathered from anywhere. There is no objection to taking cut and dried wood from a local's home or store for an army camp
4. One may carry in the army camp what is necessary, even on a Sabbath.

Carrying on the Sabbath is only permitted when a three-foot (ten handbreadths) wall is surrounding the camp. These leniencies apply from the start of a war to the army's return.

6.14 Latrines

It is forbidden to defecate in an army camp or in an open field. Instead, latrines should be built for the soldiers outside the camp,

> "Also you shall have a place outside the camp, and you shall go out there. And you shall have a tool on your staff. And it shall be, as you sit outside, you shall dig with it, and shall turn back, and shall cover that which comes from you."
> *Deuteronomy 23:12-13 KJ3*

6.15 Digging Tools

Every soldier is to have a spike hanging with his weapons. When he goes to use the latrine, he should dig a hole with the spike, relieve himself, and cover his excrement.

They must always follow these practices, whether the ark accompanies them or not,

> "For the LORD thy God walketh in the midst of thy camp, to deliver thee, and to give up thine enemies before thee; therefore shall thy camp be holy: that He see no unclean thing in thee, and turn away from thee." *Deuteronomy 23:14 KJV*

7. War Exemptions

7.1 War Priest

In both a War by Commandment and an Authorized War, a priest is appointed to address the nation before the battle begins. He is anointed with the oil of anointment and is called the War Priest.

7.2 War Priest Speech

The War Priest speaks to the nation twice. The first time is at the border, before the army leaves to assume battle positions. At that time, he tells the nation:

> "Also what man is there who has planted a vineyard and has not eaten of it? Let him go and return to his house, lest he die in the battle and another man eat of it." *Deuteronomy 20:6 NKJV*

When those who qualify hear his instructions, they return to their homes.

He speaks a second time after the army has assumed battle positions, saying:

> "And shall say unto them, Hear, O Israel, ye approach this day unto battle against your enemies: let not your hearts faint, fear not, and do not tremble, neither be ye terrified because of them." *Deuteronomy 20:3*

7.3 War Priest, Priests, and Officers

When the army is ready to enter the battle, right before they attack, the War Priest stands elevated before the array of the entire army and speaks to them in Hebrew:

> "And shall say unto them, Hear, O Israel, ye approach this day unto battle against your enemies: let not your hearts faint, fear not, and do not tremble, neither be ye terrified because of them; For the LORD your God *is* He that goeth with you, to fight for you against your enemies, to save you."
> *Deuteronomy 20:3-4*

After the War Priest finishes speaking, another priest of a lower rank reiterates the same points to the people in a loud voice. Then the War Priest says:

> "What man *is there* that hath built a new house, and hath not dedicated it? let him go and return to his house... What man *is he* that hath planted a vineyard, and hath not *yet* eaten of it? let him *also* go and return unto his house… What man *is there* that hath betrothed a wife, and hath not taken her? let him go and return unto his house…"
> *Deuteronomy 20:5-7 KJV*

After the War Priest finishes, a commander reiterates the same points to the nation in a loud voice. Then the commander speaks on his own: "'Is there anyone who is afraid or faint-hearted? Let him go home...' (Dt. 20:8).

Then a lower ranking officer proclaims the same to the people.

7.4a Preventing AWOL

After everyone has had a chance to leave the battlefront, the army is arrayed again, and commanding officers are appointed at the head of the nation.

Officers equipped with iron axes are placed in the rear of battalion. They have permission to chop off the legs of anyone fleeing the battle, because flight brings defeat.

7.4b No Exemptions for a War by Commandment

These options of leaving the battle only apply to an Authorized War. In a War by Commandment, the *entire nation, both men and women, must go* out to war, even the grooms and brides.

7.5 Building

Those who may leave the battlefront include those who build structures fit to live in including a:

1. house,
2. barn for his cattle,
3. woodshed, or
4. storage house.

A person who builds, buys, receives as a present, or inherits, a home is deferred from military service. They should return from the front.

However, one who builds a silo, gatehouse, gazebo, porch, or a house that is less than four cubits square, or a person who steals a house, does not return from the war.

7.6 Vineyards

Those deferred from military service are:

1. one who plants a vineyard
2. one who buys a vineyard
3. one who inherits a vineyard
4. one who receives a vineyard as a present
5. one who plants five fruit trees (even if different species)
6. one who grafts or extends a vineyard.

The extensions and grafts must be significant enough to obligate the vine in *orlah*.

A person is not deferred from military service if they:

1. plant four fruit trees
2. plant five or more trees that do not bear fruit
3. steal a vineyard
4. plant a vineyard with a partner.

Commentary on 7.6
Orlah is the command not to eat fruit from a tree during the first three years of fruit bearing.

7.7 Marriage in Wartime

A man is deferred from military service if he consecrates a virgin, widow, or performs the brother-in-law rite. Even if there are five brothers and one of them dies, all should return from the battlefront.

If a man consecrates [betroths] a wife on the condition that the wedding ceremony [Kiddushin] take place later at a specified date, and the contracted date occurs during a war, the man is sent home from the battlefront.

Commentary on 7.7
The brother-in-law rite is referred to in Deuteronomy 25:5.

7.8 Marriage Exceptions in Wartime

Whoever consecrates a woman whom he is forbidden to marry shall not return from the battlefield. These are:

1. Anyone who remarries his divorcee
2. High priest who marries a widow
3. A priest who marries a divorcee
4. A priest who marries a *Chalitah* Israelitess
5. An Israelite who marries a *Mamzer* or *Natinah*
6. An Israelitess who marries a *Mamzer* or *Natin.*

Commentary on 7.8
Chalitah: a Israelitess whose husband has died; but she has refused children by her brother-in-law.
Mamzer: someone born out of adultery or incest.
Natin: a descendant of the Gibeonites. ~ female Natin: Natinah.

7.9 Support in Wartime

Upon the proclamation of the priest, those who were exempted from the army camp must return to support their brethren by bringing them food, water, and other needs.

7.10 Exemption from Army Obligations

The following are exempt from all obligations related to serving in the army or supporting the troops:

1. one who builds a house and dedicates it
2. one who marries the woman he consecrated
3. one who performs the rite of the brother-in-law
4. one who redeems his vineyard.

They are not conscripted until the completion of one year.

> "When a man hath taken a new wife, he shall not go out to war, neither shall he be charged with any business: *but* he shall be free at home one year, and shall cheer up his wife which he hath taken." *Deuteronomy 24:5*

The Oral Tradition says that the one-year deferment is for one who has purchased a house, married a woman, or began to benefit from the fruit of his vineyard.

Commentary on 7.10
In this case "consecrated" means betrothed.

7.11 First Year Obligations

During the first year of obligations, he is not obligated to supply the troops with food or water, fix the roads, guard the walls, or pay the levy for beams for the gates of the city.

> "When a man hath taken a new wife, he shall not go out to war, neither shall he be charged with any business: *but* he shall be free at home one year, and shall cheer up his wife which he hath taken." *Deuteronomy 24:5*

Since the prohibition is repeated, that shows there are actually two prohibitions: he is not obligated to his city, or to the army.

7.12 Exemptions in Renting

When a person builds a house, and rents it to others, if the renters pay upfront, the owner has already benefited from it. If the renters do not pay him rent until after twelve months have passed, the owner has not benefitted from it.

7.13 House Building in Wartime

If a man must guard his belongings locked up inside of a house he built, then he has derived benefit from it. He is legally seen as dwelling there. If he does not have to guard his possessions, he is legally seen as not having derived any benefit from his home yet.

7.14 Houses Outside of Israel

Anyone who builds a house or plants a vineyard outside of the land of Israel is not sent back from the battle.

7.15 Bravery Merits Eternal Life (Sage's Additions)

The phrase "Is there a man who is afraid or faint-hearted" refers to a person who is not brave enough to fight in battle. Once a soldier enters the battle, he should trust on the Hope of Israel and *His Savior*. He must realize that he is fighting for God and the oneness of His Name. Therefore, he should place his trust in God and not show fear. He should not worry about his wife or children. Instead he should not focus on anything except the war.

Anyone who worries to the point he becomes frightened violates the commandment,

> "Let not your hearts faint, fear not, and do not tremble, neither be ye terrified because of them;" *Deuteronomy 20:3*

He can also be held responsible for the blood of the entire Jewish nation. If he does not wage war with all his heart and soul, it is considered as if he shed the blood of the entire people.

> "What man *is there that is* fearful and fainthearted? let him go and return unto his house, lest his brethren's heart faint as well as his heart." *Deuteronomy 20:8*

The prophet also says:

> "Cursed *be* he that doeth the work of the LORD deceitfully, and cursed *be* he that keepeth back his sword from blood." *Jeremiah 48:10*

In contrast, anyone who fights with his entire heart, showing no fear, with the intention of sanctifying God's name alone, can be assured that he will not be harmed. He will be granted the right to have a proper family in the land of Israel and gather merit for himself and his descendants eternally. He will also merit eternal life in the world to come,

> "For the LORD will certainly make my lord a sure house; because my lord fighteth the battles of the LORD, and evil hath not been found in thee *all* thy days. Yet a man is risen to pursue thee, and to seek thy soul: but the soul of my lord shall be bound in the bundle of life with the LORD thy God; and the souls of thine enemies, them shall He sling out, *as out* of the middle of a sling." *1 Samuel 25:28-29*

Commentary on 7.15
This is another section that was added to the original by later rabbis. We have already been told that an Israelite warrior needs to be brave for God, his country, and his people. Now the sages are reiterating that point and adding that those who fight will be protected and be granted eternal life. This sounds a lot like the Muslim idea of salvation through Jihad. Again, a person can only obtain eternal life by accepting Jesus the Messiah as his Lord and Savior as taught in

the New Testament. Notice also that Jeremiah, which was written long after the time of Samuel, is quoted.

8. Gentile-Jewish Relations

8.1 Gentile Food

When Israelite troops enter Gentile territory to conquer and take prisoners, if they become hungry and can only find forbidden food, they are permitted to eat:

1. Unproperly slaughtered animals
2. Animals that died of themselves
3. The flesh of pigs and other unclean animals.

Likewise, they may drink wine used in idol worship. This license is derived by the Oral Tradition which interprets the "good things" of Deuteronomy 6:10-11 as "pigs' necks and the like."

> "And it shall be, when the LORD thy God shall have brought thee into the land which He sware unto thy fathers, to Abraham, to Isaac, and to Jacob, to give thee great and goodly cities, which thou buildedst not, And houses full of all good *things*, which thou filledst not, and wells digged, which thou diggedst not, vineyards and olive trees, which thou plantedst not; when thou shalt have eaten and be full;" *Deuteronomy 6:10-11*

Commentary on 8.1
Jews are forbidden to eat non-kosher food. But this tells us in a war situation any food is good. Also notice, pork is "good food" which means the kosher prohibition is not for health reasons but ceremonial. See *Ancient Epistle of Barnabas 10* and the section at the end of this book entitled *Food Laws.*

8.2 Foreign Brides

A soldier may have sexual relations with a woman while she is still a Gentile if his natural inclination overcomes him. But he must bring her into his home. It is forbidden to have sexual relations with her and then just walk away.

> "And seest among the captives a beautiful woman, and hast a desire unto her, that thou wouldest have her to thy wife; Then thou shalt bring her home to thine house; and she shall shave her head, and pare her nails;" *Deuteronomy 21:11-12*

He is forbidden to have sexual relations with her a second time until he marries her.

Commentary on 8.2
It is sin to have sexual relations with anyone and not marry them. If the soldier does have sex with a Gentile, he must take her home and marry her immediately. She then has twelve months to fully convert to Judaism, or the marriage is null and void.

8.3 Sexual Relations with Canaanite Women

Sexual relations with a woman captive is only permitted while she is in captivity as the verse states "If you see... among the prisoners."

This marriage license is permitted whether the woman is a virgin or not. It can even be granted if she is married, because the Gentiles' marriages are not recognized.

Several laws can be seen in the passage of Deuteronomy quoted above:

- "And you have a desire" – even though she is not beautiful.
- "Her" – and not another. He may not engage in sexual relations with two women.
- "You would have her as a wife" – He may not take two captives, one for himself and another for his father or brother.

He may not pressure her in the midst of the war,

> "Then thou shalt bring her home to thine house; and she shall shave her head, and pare her nails;" *Deuteronomy 21:12*

He must first bring her into a private place, and then engage in relations with her.

Commentary on 8.3
Canaanite Gentiles did not have marriage licenses. Therefore, their marriages could never be proven. If she wanted to leave, she could.

8.4 Priests and Canaanite Women (Sage's Additions)

The sages taught that a priest is allowed relations with a woman captive; but the Torah only permits relations as a concession to man's natural inclination. However, he is not permitted to marry her afterwards, because priests are forbidden to marry converts.

> **Commentary on 8.4**
> Concubines are only allowed for kings, not common men, see 4:4. Apparently, they were later allowed for priests also. Her children would never be allowed into the priesthood. Jesus stated that these types of laws were because of the hardness of men's hearts and should not exist. See Matthew 19:8.

8.5 Relations Before Conversion (Sage's Additions)

Once a Jew has had relations with a woman captive and brought her to his home, if she wants to convert to Judaism, she must be baptized for conversion immediately.

If she does not wish to become a Jewess, she should dwell in his house for thirty days. She should mourn the abandonment of her faith. Her captor should not keep her from mourning.

> "And she shall put the raiment of her captivity from off her, and shall remain in thine house, and bewail her father and her mother a full month: and after that thou shalt go in unto her, and be her husband, and she shall be thy wife." *Deuteronomy 21:13*

The sages taught that she must let her nails grow and shave her head so that she will not appear attractive to him. She must be together with him at home. Thus, when he enters, he sees her; and when he leaves, he sees her, so that he becomes disgusted with her.

Commentary on 8.5
A Jew may marry a non-convert only if she agrees to fully convert within one year. Otherwise she must depart. Again, the explanation from the sages shows their complete lack of understanding true circumcision of the heart.

8.6 Marrying a Canaanite Woman

A captor must give his captive three months: the month of mourning plus the two months following it. At the end of the three months if they decide to get married, he must give her a *Kiddushin* and a *Ketubah.* If he does not desire her, he must set her free. If he sells her, he violates a negative commandment,

> "And it shall be, if thou have no delight in her, then thou shalt let her go whither she will; but thou shalt not sell her at all for money, thou shalt not make merchandise of her, because thou hast humbled her." *Deuteronomy 21:14*

Should a captor sell his captive, the sale is invalid, and the money must be returned.

Likewise, he is forbidden to force her to work as a servant [make merchandise] after he has had relations with her.

Commentary on 8.6
If the Gentile woman captive changes her mind about converting to Judaism or either the man or woman changes their minds about getting married; then the Gentile woman captive must go free. She is not his daughter to marry off. He cannot accept a bride price.

8.7 Conversion of a Captive ~ Noahide or Jewess

The captive is given twelve months to decide to become a Jew or a Noahide. If she does not desire to convert to Judaism after the twelve months, she must, at least, agree to accept the seven universal laws commanded to Noah's descendants. If she becomes a Noahide, she is set free. Her status is the same as all other resident aliens. He may not marry her, for a Jew is forbidden to marry a Gentile.

Commentary on 8.7
All resident aliens are Noahides.

8.8 Children of a Captive

If she conceives after the initial relations with her captor, the child is regarded as a convert. The child is not deemed the captor's son, because his mother is a Gentile. Instead, the court baptizes and takes responsibility for him.

Tamar was conceived from King David's initial relations with a woman captive, but Absalom was conceived after their marriage. Thus, Tamar was only Absalom's maternal sister and would have been permitted to marry Amnon.

> "I pray thee, speak unto the king; for he will not withhold me from thee." *2 Samuel 13:13*

Commentary on 8.8

Princess Maachah
Maachah, was the daughter of king Talmai of Geshur, wife of King David, mother of Tamar and Absalom. When she married King David she had the status of a "captive woman" or a non-convert. She would have been given twelve months to learn the Jewish ways and fully convert.

Absalom
Absalom was the son of King David and Princess Maachah of Geshur. He was born after the first twelve months, making him a full Jew by birth. Absalom could not have Tamar as a wife since they were brother and sister by the same mother.

Tamar
Tamar was the daughter of King David and princess Maachah of Geshur. She was born during the first twelve months, making her a convert by court. This means when she reached the age of accountability she had the option of converting to Judaism, becoming a Noahide, or leaving the country if she wished to be an idolater.

Amnon
Amnon was the son of King David and Ahinoam the Jezreelitess. Amnon could have had Tamar as a wife because they were not brother and sister from the same mother. Section 8.8 seems to be saying since she was a convert by court, she would have been considered the legal daughter of King David for marriage purposes.

Section 8.8 may be a later addition to the Law. Notice it quotes 2 Samuel, which would have been after Samuel wrote the Law of Kings.

8.9 Abandonment of Idol Worship

A woman captive who refuses to abandon idol worship within the twelve-month period and does not leave Israel shall be executed. Also, Israel cannot make a treaty with any [Canaanite] city which desires to accept the peaceful settlement, unless they first repent of idolatry by destroying their places of pagan worship and accept the seven universal laws commanded of Noah's descendants. In any city where Israel has undisputed authority, every Gentile who does not accept these commandments will be executed.

Commentary on 8.9
Abandonment of idolatry is mandatory for achieving "peaceful settlement" in Israel.

8.10 Israelites and Noahides

Moses gave the Torah and the Commandments only to Israel for an inheritance, and to all those from among the other nations who want to convert.

> "Moses commanded us a law, *even* the inheritance of the congregation of Jacob." *Deuteronomy 33:4*

> "One ordinance *shall be both* for you of the congregation, and also for the stranger that sojourneth *with you*, an ordinance forever in your generations: as ye *are*, so shall the stranger be before the LORD." *Numbers 15:15*

No one should be forced to accept the Torah and the Commandments unless they are called by God to do so. However, God commanded Moses to *compel* all the nations of the world to accept the laws given to Noah's descendants. Anyone who refuses these commands shall be executed. Anyone who officially accepts these commands is referred to as a "resident alien." This can take place anywhere; but must be made before a board of three Torah scholars.

Anyone who vows to have himself circumcised has twelve months to perform the rite or he is considered as one of the nations.

> **Commentary on 8.10**
> Every nation must follow the moral laws of God (Noahide laws); but the Law of Moses was given to the Jews and those living in the land of Israel. Other nations must be believers; but not necessarily follow the Mosaic law.

8.11 Devotion to God

Anyone who accepts these seven commands and seriously observes them is considered one of "the pious among the Gentiles" and will merit a share in the world to come. This only applies when he accepts and fulfills them because he wants to please the Holy One in the way that the Torah commands. Moses, our teacher, has informed us that Noah had originally given these commands to all his descendants [Genesis 9].

However, if he only fulfills them for the sake of peace, he is not a resident alien, nor of "the pious among the Gentiles," nor one of their wise men.

> **Commentary on 8.11**
> Keeping the seven laws merits eternal life only in the sense that if you keep commands one and two (see the next chapter), you would be worshiping the God of Israel and awaiting the prophecy of the

coming of the Messiah to be fulfilled. When the Messiah did reveal Himself as explained in Daniel 9:26 (Messiah came before Titus destroyed the Jerusalem temple) and in this book in 11.1, you would have become His follower, a Christian.

The Seven Noahide Laws

1. ABSTAIN FROM IDOLATRY
2. DO NOT COMMIT BLASPHEMY
3. DO NOT COMMIT MURDER
4. DO NOT COMMIT FORNICATION
5. DO NOT STEAL
6. DO NOT EAT BLOOD
7. ESTABLISH COURTS OF JUSTICE

9. Seven Noahide Laws

9.1 History – the Six Adamic Laws

God commanded Adam to observe these six precepts:

1. Abstain from idolatry
2. Do not commit blasphemy
3. Do not commit murder
4. Do not commit fornication
5. Do not steal
6. Establish laws and courts of justice.

Even though Moses gave all these self-evident laws, the Torah [Talmud] teaches that Adam codified these laws.

Noah added the prohibition against eating flesh from a living animal:

> "But flesh with the life thereof, *which is* the blood thereof, shall ye not eat." *Genesis 9:4*

This created the seven Noahide Laws.

These laws remained the same throughout history until the time of Abraham. When Abraham arose, in addition to these seven laws, God commanded him regarding circumcision. Abraham also ordained the morning prayers.

Isaac separated tithes and ordained an evening prayer service. Jacob added the prohibition against eating the sciatic nerve and re-ordained the evening prayers. Amram added other commands while in Egypt. Finally, Moses completed the Torah.

Commentary on 9.1

Genesis 9 is the chapter that deals with the Noahide Covenant.

Ge. 9:1, 7 Fornication is wrong because we need healthy children.
Ge. 9:3 Gentiles can eat any meat (kosher and non-kosher).
Ge. 9:4 Eating flesh from a living animal is forbidden.
Ge. 9:6 Murder is wrong; and we need courts of justice.
Ge. 9:8-9 There is only one true God, and this is His covenant.
Ge. 9:9 Gentile law is for all nations.
Ge. 9:13 The rainbow is the sign of the Noahide Covenant.
Ge. 9:16 The Noahide Covenant is a perpetual covenant.

The fact that God destroyed the earth with a flood proves that humanity disobeyed the laws God gave to Adam.

The Ancient Book of Jubilees 6:24, records that Noah also ordained four feasts at the solstices and equinoxes as *days of remembrance* of the flood and for repentance.

9.2 First Law – Idolatry

A Gentile is held guilty of idolatry if he is intentionally worshiping false gods in an accepted manner.

A Gentile would be executed in a Noahide court for every type of idolatry in which a Jewish court would execute him. If a Jewish court would not execute him, then neither would a Noahide Court. They are the same laws. Even if a Gentile would not be executed for certain types of idolatry, he is still forbidden to participate in any form of idolatry. He would not be allowed to erect a monument, plant an Asherah, or to make images, even if they are only for the sake of beauty.

Commentary on 9.2
We must acknowledge that there is only one God (revealing Himself as a trinity; Noahides call this "partnership"). We must avoid anything associated with idols and idolatry. Even if something looks like an idol or image, but it's just decorative, it is still forbidden. It might be a stumbling block to someone and we need our Christian witness to be pure. See the appendix on Idolatry for a detailed discussion about what constitutes idolatry from the section of the Mishnah called the *Avodah Zarah.*

9.3 Second Law – Blasphemy

A Gentile who curses God's Name, (including His actual name and/or His titles), in any language, is guilty.

Commentary on 9.3
We show God respect by not cursing in His name or repeating lies (false doctrine) about Him. This requires that we study His law and the prophesies He has given, specifically about the Messiah. We blaspheme by calling God a liar by our actions or by teaching what is contradictory to the Word of God. In the following verses, the Jews claimed Jesus blasphemed by teaching He was the Messiah; but they blasphemed by rejecting Him as the Messiah.

> "Again the high priest asked Him, and said unto Him, Art Thou the Christ, the Son of the Blessed? And Jesus said, I am… Then the high priest rent his clothes, and saith, What need we any further witnesses? Ye have heard the blasphemy: what think ye? And they all condemned Him to be guilty of death." *Mark 14:61-64*

> "The Jews answered Him, saying, for a good work we stone Thee not; but for blasphemy; and because that Thou, being a man, makest Thyself God." *John 10:33*

> "…blasphemy *against* the *Holy* Ghost shall not be forgiven unto men." *Matthew 12:31b*

To disbelieve the words of this covenant and ignore the words of Noah is the same thing as saying God lied, which amounts to blasphemy. We must believe in the predictions given by Noah, and later Moses, about the coming of Messiah, and we must accept Him when He comes. To not study the prophecies and look for the Messiah amounts to blasphemy!

9.4 Third Law – Murder

A Gentile who murders anyone, even an unborn child, should be executed as the penalty for their crime. Likewise, he is guilty if he murdered a person who was on their deathbed, placed a person before a lion, or starved a person to death. He should be executed because he murdered in one way or another.

Likewise, a person who kills someone who attacked another person when he could have wounded the attacker, or stopped them in another way, shall be executed.

Commentary on 9.4

Premeditated murder, abortion, and euthanasia are capital offences. Self-defense and the defense of others is required. For manslaughter see 10.1.

> "Then said He unto them, But now, he that hath a purse, let him take *it*, and likewise *his* scrip: and he that hath no sword, let him sell his garment, and buy one." *Luke 22:36*

> "But if any provide not for his own, and specially for those of his own house, he hath denied the faith, and is worse than an infidel." *1 Timothy 5:8*

9.5 Fourth Law – Fornication

Gentiles are forbidden six illicit sexual relations:

1. His father's wife
2. His mother
3. A married woman
4. A male
5. An animal
6. His maternal sister.

These prohibitions are inferred from this verse in Genesis:

> "Therefore shall a man leave his father and his mother, and shall cleave unto his wife: and they shall be one flesh." *Genesis 2:24*

1. "His father" – he cannot marry his father's wife
2. "His mother" – he cannot marry his mother
3. "cleave to his wife" – he cannot marry another's wife
4. "his wife" – he cannot marry a male
5. "They shall be one flesh" – bestiality is forbidden (no man can become "one flesh" with an animal.)

The prohibition against relations with a maternal sister can be derived from:

> "And yet indeed *she is* my sister; she *is* the daughter of my father, but not the daughter of my mother; and she became my wife." *Genesis 20:12*

Commentary on 9.5
Fornication is defined as committing incest, adultery, cohabitation, homosexually, or bestiality. It is forbidden to have sex with anyone you have not married or cannot legally marry. Having a child is creating one new flesh out of the two of you.

9.6 Fornication Clarified

A Gentile is liable for relations with:

1. His mother, even if she was seduced or raped by his father and never married to him. She is still his biological mother
2. His father's wife, even after his father's death
3. A male, whether a minor or an adult
4. An animal, whether young or old

For bestiality: A Gentile is executed, but not the animal. A Jew is executed along with the animal.

9.7a Gentile Adultery

A Gentile is not executed for adultery with another Gentile's wife unless they engage in relations in the normal manner after she has consummated her marriage.

> "But God came to Abimelech in a dream by night, and said to him, Behold, thou *art but* a dead man, for the woman which thou hast taken; for she is a man's wife." *Genesis 20:3*

Commentary on 9.7a
A Gentile is executed for adultery. If she has not consummated the marriage, she is still free to change her mind and get the marriage annulled.

9.7b Jewish Adultery

A Gentile who has relations with a married Jewess is liable for the death penalty whether they had normal or abnormal relations.

A Gentile who has relations with a betrothed Jewish maiden is stoned to death according to Jewish law.

If he had relations with her after her wedding, but before she consummated the marriage, he is strangled to death according to Jewish law.

If he has relations with a Jewish woman after she consummated her marriage, he is decapitated as if he had engaged in relations with a married Gentile woman.

Commentary on 9.7b
I am unsure of the legal definitions of normal and abnormal relations.

9.8 Gentile Divorce

A Gentile who gives one of his maid-servants to marry one of his servants, then engages in relations with her, is executed for committing adultery with her. However, he is only liable after she has become publicly known [officially married] as the wife of the servant.

He may have relations with her when she separates from her husband and shows herself in public with her hair uncovered. [This was the way Gentile women showed they were divorced.]

Gentiles have no formal written divorce proceedings. A Gentile woman is considered divorced when:

1. her husband removes her from his home and sends her on her own, or
2. she leaves his domain and goes her own way.

Divorce is not dependent on the man's discretion alone. If either the husband or wife decides to separate, they may, and then they are no longer considered married.

Commentary on 9.8
Both husband and wife have equal rights. Either can initiate a divorce by separating. This is why the apostle Paul says a believer is not under bondage in the case of an unbeliever leaving them (1 Corinthians 7:15). Christian law decrees if both husband and wife are believers, there is never to be a divorce (Matthew 19:5-6). In the *Testament of Noah* (Dead Sea Scrolls), Noah testified that he married his wife "according to the marriage custom that the Lord of Eternity gave to Adam." So, we know that from the beginning there were supposed to be marriage licenses. If going out in public with your head uncovered shows you are divorced (no longer under the authority of your husband) then this might be the reason why the apostle Paul says, in 1 Corinthians 11:5, that wives should have their head covered when praying or prophesying in church.

9.9 Fifth Law – Theft

A Gentile is liable for theft whether he stole from a Jew or a Gentile. This applies to:

Ancient Law of Kings

1. Forceful robbery
2. Stealing when no one is looking
3. Kidnapping a person
4. Withholding an employee's wages
5. A worker who eats from his employer's produce when he is not working.

In these cases, he is held guilty as a robber. The law is different for Jews. Likewise, a Gentile is held guilty for stealing anything, even if it is worth less than a *p'rutah* [smallest coin]. If one Gentile stole such an object and another Gentile stole it from him, they are both to be executed.

> **Commentary on 9.9**
> Louis Ginsberg's Legends of the Jews II records a dialog between Joseph and his brothers about Joseph's supposedly stolen divining cup. It is stated that Hebrew law makes a thief pay back two times the price of the object stolen. Only if he cannot pay, is he put into a debtor's prison. Gentile law, on the other hand, states that the thief can be deprived of all he owns; but cannot be executed if that is enough to pay the debt.

9.10 Sixth Law – Severed Limb and Blood

A Gentile may not eat a limb or flesh from a living animal, regardless of the amount involved. The specification of minimum amounts only applies to Jews. A Gentile is permitted to consume blood from a living creature. Jews are not.

Commentary on 9.10
Genesis 9:4 is often believed to say Gentiles cannot eat blood. But it is actually saying that Gentiles cannot eat living animals, or part of an animal while it is still alive. In Leviticus 17:12, Jews and Gentiles who live in Israel are forbidden to consume blood.

9.11 Severed Limb – Domesticated or Wild

The prohibition against eating a limb or flesh from a living animal pertains to both domesticated animals and wild beasts.

9.12 Severed Limb – Kosher or Not

Even if an animal is slaughtered in the kosher way; a Gentile cannot eat any flesh cut off the animal while it was still moving.

9.13 Severed Limb – Jew and Gentile

Jews and Gentiles alike are forbidden to eat meat cut from a living animal, but they differ in two instances: a Jew cannot eat non-kosher food even if it was slaughtered properly, but a Gentile can. A Jew may take small portions of flesh cut from a living animal if the two signs of life are severed [in the process of dying], even if the animal is still moving. Gentiles may not.

9.14 Seventh Law – Courts of Justice

Gentiles are obligated to set up courts with police in every major city to insure justice concerning these first six commands and to warn the people to observe them.

A Gentile who breaks one of these seven commands shall be executed by decapitation. This is why all the Shechemites were executed. The people knew that Shechem kidnapped Dinah; but did not take him to court.

A Gentile is executed on the basis of the testimony of one witness and the verdict of a single judge. No warning is required. Relatives may serve as witnesses. However, a wife may not serve as a witness or sit in judgment of her husband.

Commentary on 9.14
A thief may not be executed. See commentary on 9.9
The event of the Shechemites is recorded in Genesis 34:1-31

10. Exceptions

10.1 Inadvertent Violation

A Gentile who accidently violates one of his laws is exempt from any punishment except for manslaughter. In the case of manslaughter, the court will not execute him; but he cannot flee to a city of refuge and the redeemer of blood is free to kill him.

This only applies when he violates a command without sinful intention. One example is someone who has relations with another Gentile's wife under the impression that she is his own wife, or she is unmarried. However, if he knew that she was another Gentile's wife, or knew she was not available, he is held responsible. Another example is a Gentile who did not know the manner in which he killed was forbidden, or he did know that he did not the authority to kill in the area the incident happened in. In these cases, the actions of the Gentile are not considered as unintentional and he is executed. These are not inadvertent violations. He did not take the time to learn the laws that apply to him.

Commentary on 10.1

If a man thought a woman was officially separated from her Gentile husband, but she lied to him, or another man said he had betrothed her; it was the man's responsibility to make sure of the specific laws on that in the country he was in at the time.

This also applies to those who had the legal right to kill in their native country, but that right is not granted in the country or jurisdiction they were in when they killed someone.

10.2 Coercion

A Gentile who is forced to violate one of his commandments shall not be punished, even if he is forced into idolatry. Gentiles are not commanded to sanctify God's name. A Gentile minor, deaf-mute, or fool is never punished because the commandments are not binding on them.

10.3 Reversing Conversion Forbidden

A Gentile who converts to Judaism, is circumcised, and is baptized, then decides to convert back to the status of a resident alien, is not permitted to do so. Instead, he must remain as an Israelite in all matters or be executed.

If a minor who was baptized by the court wishes to repudiate his conversion when he attains the age of accountability and assume the status of a resident alien [*Ger Toshav*], he may. However, if he does not object immediately upon entering the age of accountability, he no longer has that option, and his status remains that of a righteous convert [*Ger Tzedek*].

If a Jew has relations with a minor girl who was baptized by a court, the money due her as payment of her *ketubah* or as a fine for raping or seducing her is held by the court until she attains lawful age. This is to make sure she does not take the money and repudiate her conversion. If she did so, she would derive benefit as a Gentile from monies to which she would only be entitled *to* if she stayed a convert, according to Jewish law.

Commentary on 10.4
The following order is the status of the worst to the best possible social order according to Judaism:

1. *Acum* (idolater)
2. *Nochri* (neither an idolater nor Noahide)
3. *Ger* (resident alien)
   a. *Ger Toshav* (a Noahide)
   b. *Ger Tzedek* (full Jewish convert)

10.4 Conversion and Repentance

A Gentile who converts after blaspheming God, engaging in idolatry, adultery, or killing a fellow Gentile is exempt from punishment. However, if he converts after murdering a Jew or committing adultery with a Jew's wife, he is liable. He is decapitated for murdering the Jew or strangled to death for committing adultery with a Jew's wife. He is punished by Jewish law because his status has changed.

Commentary on 10.4
Leniency may be granted for someone who might have committed crimes based on the idolatrous system his country was under. If, however, he has interacted with Jews enough, then he should have known better and may therefore be executed.

10.5 Decapitation

Gentiles are always executed by decapitation with two exceptions:

1. He is stoned for adultery with a consecrated Jewish maiden

2. He is strangled for adultery with a Jew's wife if it occurs after the marriage ceremony, but before the marriage is consummated.

Commentary on 10.5
The term "consecrated" here could mean either a betrothed woman or a woman set apart from society and dedicated to temple sevice.

10.6a Cross-Breeding

Oral tradition dictates that Gentiles are forbidden to cross-breed animals or graft different species of trees together. However, this is not a capital offence.

Commentary on 10.6a
One has to wonder if this was because of the fallen angels and their cross-breeding experiments as mentioned in the *Book of Enoch.*

10.6b Gentile Striking a Jew

A Gentile who strikes a Jew is liable for the death penalty even if he causes only minor damage. Even though this is technically a capital offence, he is not executed for it.

Commentary on 10.6b
Compare this to our laws about striking a federal officer. The word here for "strike" may mean "strike with the intent to kill."

10.7 Circumcision

Only Abraham and his descendants were commanded to be circumcised:

> "And God said unto Abraham, Thou shalt keep My covenant therefore, thou, and thy seed after thee in their generations. This is My covenant, which ye shall keep, between Me and you and thy seed after thee; Every man child among you shall be circumcised." *Genesis 17:9-10*

Ishmael's descendants are excluded:

> "for in Isaac shall thy seed be called."
> *Genesis 21:12*

Esau's descendants are also excluded:

> "And He will give the blessing of Abraham to thee, and to thy sons with thee,"
> *Genesis 28:4 Targum*

This implies that only Jacob is the true offspring of Abraham who maintains his true faith. Thus, Israel alone is obligated in circumcision.

10.8 Keturah's Sons Circumcised (Sage's Additions)
Our sages concluded that the descendants of Isaac, of Ishmael, and of Abraham and Keturah, are all obligated to be circumcised. However, present-day Ishmaelites and Keturahites are intermingled, therefore they are all obligated to be circumcised on the eighth day. However, they are not executed for failure to do so.

Commentary on 10.8
It was just stated in 10.7 that the only males who are required to be circumcised are the Israelites. In section 10.8 the sages added Keturah's children. This is not part of the original law.

10.9a Illegal Gentile Torah Observance

A Gentile who studies [observes in his own way] the Torah is obligated to die. They should only be involved in the study of their seven commandments.

Commentary on 10.9a
The Kenites, and some of the prophets, like Nathan, were Torah scholars and Noahide Gentiles and they were blessed by God for their study. A Gentile who created his own cultic teachings based on Torah is obligated to die. See 10.9c

10.9b Illegal Gentile Sabbath Observance

Likewise, a Gentile who rests, even on a weekday, observing that day as a Sabbath [doing rituals], is obligated to die. He is also guilty if he creates a religious festival for himself.

Commentary on 10.9b
It should be noted that the Messiah instituted Sunday observance. Christians and Jews had nothing to do with it. Most of the times when Jesus appeared to people during the forty days between His resurrection and ascension, the Scripture goes out of its way to point out that His appearances were on the first day of the week. See the chapter on *The Sabbath* for details.

10.9c Replacement Theology

The general principle is: Gentiles are not to be allowed to create a new religion or order for themselves based on their own decisions. They may either become righteous converts [fully convert to Judaism] and accept all the [Jewish] laws or retain Gentile law without adding or subtracting from them. If a Gentile studies the Torah, ordains a Sabbath, or creates a religious rite, a Jewish court should beat and punish him, and inform him that he is obligated to die. However, he is *not* to be executed.

Commentary on 10.9c
Neither Jews nor Gentiles should be allowed to start their own religions. A new unauthorized religion might be Rabbinic Judaism for placing Oral Torah on equal footing with Written Torah, or Karaite Judaism for rejecting Oral Torah. Another might be Kabalistic Judaism. These three systems cannot all be the "original" Judaism. At least two of these must be Jewish forms of replacement theology. God abolished temple sacrifices by allowing the temple to be destroyed. Christians and Jews had nothing to do with it. Therefore, all forms of Christian replacement theology are equally illegal, whether they are replacement theology by their doctrine alone or by incorporating Jewish temple rituals in their services.

Notice they are informed that they should die; but are punished and then sent away. This is what happened to Peter and John in Acts 4.

10.10a Legal Gentile Torah Observance

If a Gentile desires to perform one of the Torah's *mitzvot* in order to receive reward, he should be allowed to do so if he does it in the required manner. If he brings an animal to be sacrificed as a burnt offering, we should receive it.

Commentary on 10.10a
A Gentile would bring an offering into the court of the Gentiles but notice here that the sacrifice is received from the Gentile. He doesn't actually do a sacrifice himself. As Christians, we should study the

seven festivals and the Torah, but not try to practice a changed or modified version of the Mosaic Law.

10.10b Gentile Charity

If a Noahide Gentile gives charity, we should accept it from him.

10.11 Jewish Courts Oversee Gentile Courts

The Jewish court must appoint judges for the "resident aliens" to judge them according to Gentile law so that the world will not become morally corrupt. The court may appoint Gentile judges or Jewish judges for Gentile courts.

10.12 Gentile and Jewish Law Precedents

In a dispute between two resident aliens [*Ger*], if both want to be judged by Jewish law they are allowed that. However, if at least one wants to be judged by Gentile law, the case shall be judged by Gentile law.

In a dispute between a Jew and a resident alien [*Ger*], if the Jew will fare better with Gentile law, he is judged according to it. When the verdict is rendered, the judge says: "Your law obligates this judgement." If the Jew will fare better with Jewish law, he is judged according to Torah law. When the verdict is rendered, the judge says: "Our law obligates this judgement."

The sages taught that the precedent is for a resident alien [*Ger*] to be judged according to Gentile law. But regarding respect, honor and charity, a resident alien [*Ger*] is to be treated as a Jew, because Jews are commanded to support them.

> "Ye shall not eat *of* anything that dieth of itself: thou shalt give it unto the stranger [*Ger*] that is in thy gates, that he may eat it; or thou mayest sell it unto an alien [*Nochri*]:" *Deuteronomy 14:21 KJV*

Commentary on 10.12
In 8.9 unrepentant idolaters are executed. They do not sue each other in a Jewish court. In 8.11 only a Noahide can be a "resident alien" and allowed to sue someone in a Gentile or Jewish court.

Noahides are judged in a Gentile court unless there is a reason to use a Jewish court. Money from Gentiles should go to help Noahides, and money from Jews and converts should go to help Jews and converts.

The following order is the status of the worst to the best possible social order according to Judaism:

1. *Acum* (idolater)
2. *Nochri* (neither an idolater nor Noahide)
3. *Ger* (resident alien)
    a. *Ger Toshav* (a Noahide)
    b. *Ger Tzedek* (full Jewish convert)

11. The Messiah (Sage's Additions)

11.1a What Messiah Accomplishes

In the future, when King Messiah arises, He will:

1. Restore the Davidic dynasty with its sovereignty[a]
2. Build the temple
3. Gather the dispersed of Israel
4. Renew sacrifices
5. Renew the sabbatical and Jubilee years according to all their particulars as described by the Torah
6. Cause all statutes to be observed in their original way.

Anyone who does not believe in King Messiah and does not await His coming, denies not only Moses and the prophets, but the entire Torah. The Torah testifies to Messiah's coming,

> "That then the LORD thy God will turn thy captivity, and have compassion upon thee, and will return and gather thee from all the nations, whither the LORD thy God hath scattered thee. If any of thine be driven out unto the outmost *parts* of heaven, from thence will the LORD thy God gather thee, and from thence will He fetch thee: And the LORD thy God will bring thee into the land which

[a] Acts 15:16-17 – the tabernacle of David restored

> thy fathers possessed, and thou shalt possess it; and He will do thee good, and multiply thee above thy fathers." *Deuteronomy 30:3-5*

All the prophets agree with these words of the Torah.

Balaam references the coming of the Messiah when he prophecies about two anointed kings.

> "I shall see Him, but not now: I shall behold Him, but not nigh: there shall come a Star out of Jacob, and a Sceptre shall rise out of Israel, and shall smite the corners of Moab, and destroy all the children of Sheth. And Edom shall be a possession, Seir also shall be a possession for His enemies; and Israel shall do valiantly." *Numbers 24:17-18 KJV*

Commentary on 11.1a
This section was added after the destruction of the Jerusalem temple in AD 70. They are expecting the Messiah to rebuild it. The Messiah will also see that the statutes (laws and teachings) are understood correctly. That means when He comes there will be those who will stand against Him because they misunderstand the Law. They recognize two Messianic kings instead of two comings of the same Messiah.

11.1b Balaam's Prophecy

The first anointed king is David who saved Israel from her oppressors. The second is King Messiah who arises from David's descendants to save Israel in the end of days. Numbers 24:17-18 can be broken down like this:

1. "I see Him, but not now" – refers to David
2. "I behold Him, but not nigh" – refers to Messiah
3. "A star out of Jacob" – refers to David
4. "A Sceptre shall rise out of Israel" – refers to Messiah
5. "smite Moab" – refers to David, "He smote Moab and measured them with a line;" *2 Samuel 8:2*
6. "destroy all the children of Sheth" – refers to Messiah ~ "He will rule from sea to sea." *Zechariah 9:10*
7. "Edom will be possession" – refers to David, "Edom became the servants of David;" *2 Samuel 8:6*
8. "Seir will be His enemies' possession" – refers to Messiah, "Saviors shall come up on mount Zion to judge the mount of Esau...." *Obadiah 1:21*

Commentary on 11.1b
David did subjugate the Moabites. The Hebrew word "Sheth" means a "tumult," and since it is used with Moab, Edom, and Seir, it most likely means anti-Messianic (Islamic) nations. When the Messiah returns the area of Mt Seir (Jordan and Saudi Arabia), it will be a stronghold for His enemies (Islam).

Notice in trying to prove point six is messianic, they quote Zechariah 10:9-10. They know one of the signs of the Messiah is that He will enter Jerusalem riding on a donkey!

11.2 Three New Cities of Refuge

Likewise, three more cities of refuge will be added: Deuteronomy 19:8-9 states: "When God will expand your borders... you must add three more cities." This command was never fulfilled. Therefore, the Messiah will achieve this because God's word is never in vain.

There are too many predictions about the Messiah to be cited here. The books of the prophets are filled with them.

11.3a Proof by Miracles

It is not true that King Messiah must work miracles like resurrecting the dead or bringing new things into the world.

Rabbi Akiba, one of the greatest sages of the period of the Mishna, supported Simon bar Kokhba and taught Bar Kokhba was King Messiah. Not only Rabbi Akiba, but all the sages of that time believed that Bar Kokhba was the Messiah until he was killed for his own sins. Only after Bar Kokhba's death did everyone realize he was not the Messiah.

Since the sages did not ask him to do any signs or miracles, that proves that King Messiah is not expected to do them.

> **Commentary on 11.3a**
> So the sages are saying that the Messiah does not have to prove Himself by doing miracles. *All* of the wisest Rabbis fell for a false messiah because they did not demand a sign as rabbis did in the days of Jesus of Nazareth (Mark 8:11-12). Their line of reasoning is illogical.

11.3b Changing the Torah

This is the main point: this Torah, with its statutes and laws, is everlasting. We may not add to it or take away from it.

Commentary on 11.3b
We may not take away or add to the Bible, but it has already been stated in 11.1a that the Messiah will change Torah observance back to the way it was supposed to be when He comes. This proves that their current understanding and observance of Torah is in error!

11.4a King Messiah Does Not Die

When a descendant of King David arises who seriously studies and observes both the Oral and Written Torah, and leads all of Israel into following Torah by rectifying the breaches in its observance, and fighting the wars of God, we may consider Him the Messiah.

If He is successful in this, then builds the Jerusalem temple, and gathers the dispersed of Israel, He would definitely be the Messiah.

The Messiah will move all nations of the world to serve God together.

> "For then will I turn to the people a pure language,
> that they may all call upon the name of the LORD,
> to serve Him with one consent." *Zephaniah 3:9*

If the descendant of David does not do these things or is killed, he cannot be the Redeemer the Torah promises. Instead, he should be considered as just a godly king of the Davidic dynasty who died. God allowed him to arise only to test the people.

> "Even some of the wise will stumble, so that they may be refined, purified and made spotless until the time of the end – for it will still come at the appointed time." *Daniel 11:35 TLV*

Commentary on 11.4a
The apostles taught the "breeches of the tabernacle of David" were restored by the Jerusalem Council of AD 50. See Acts 15:16.

Daniel 9 shows that before the Second Coming of Jesus Christ, a false messiah will do exactly that: rebuild the Jerusalem temple and proclaim himself the Messiah. Taking this portion literally without knowing the New Testament would lead one to accept the Antichrist as the promised Messiah.

By their definition, Jesus of Nazareth who was a king from David's line did these things, except that He died; therefore, Jesus is a godly king. A godly king would not lie by saying He was the Messiah when He was not.

That also means God tested Israel with Bar Kokhba and they failed.

11.4b Jesus of Nazareth

Jesus of Nazareth, who claimed to be the Messiah, was executed by the Sanhedrin. The prophet Daniel alluded to Jesus saying:

> "The vulgar among your people shall exalt themselves in an attempt to fulfill the vision, but they shall stumble."
> *Daniel 11:14 (badly paraphrased)*

All the prophets called the Messiah the Redeemer of Israel and their Savior who would gather their dispersed and strengthen their observance of Torah commands. Christianity is the biggest obstacle to this because it has caused the Jews to be slain, scattered, and humbled. It has caused Torah to be altered, and most of the world to fall away by serving a false god.

Nevertheless, we cannot completely understand the ways of the Creator.

> "For My thoughts *are* not your thoughts, neither *are* your ways My ways, saith the LORD. For *as* the heavens are higher than the earth, so are My ways higher than your ways, and My thoughts than your thoughts." *Isaiah 55:8-9*

Ultimately, all the deeds of Jesus of Nazareth, and of that Ishmaelite [Muhammad] who came after Him, will prepare the way for Messiah's coming, which will improve the entire world, motivating all nations to serve God together.

> "For then will I turn to the people a pure language, that they may all call upon the name of the LORD, to serve Him with one consent." *Zephaniah 3:9*

Commentary on 11.4b
They deliberately left out the first part of Daniel 11:14, which says "And in those times there shall many stand up against the king of the south: also..." This verse is referring to the wars that occur during the reign of Ptolemy V Epiphanes (203-181 BC), two hundred years before the time of Jesus of Nazareth!

11.4c The World's Misunderstanding of Torah

How will this come about? The entire world, from the smallest islands to the most stubborn of nations, has heard about the Messiah, the Torah, and the commandments.

Some take one side saying, "The commandments were true but have been annulled for this age. They were only temporary."

Others say, "The Messiah has already come and revealed the hidden spiritual truths of the commandments. We are not to take them literally."

When the real Messiah comes, and fulfills His mission and is exalted, they will all come to realize that their ancestors taught them a false history and their prophets and ancestors led them into error.

Commentary on 11.4c

These are forms of replacement theology. The apostle Paul did say the priesthood and law changes back to the Melchizedekian priesthood and law. There are those who think Paul meant that we are free to break moral (Gentile) law. The Dead Sea Scrolls teach that the Messiah changes the priesthood and law. See *Ancient Testaments of the Patriarchs*.

12. The Messianic Age (Sage's Additions)

12.1 Messiah Brings Peace

In the Messianic age the world's nature will not change nor will the creatures of this world change. Everything will continue according to its pattern.

Although Isaiah 11:6 states:

> "In the days of the Messiah of Israel peace shall be multiplied in the earth. The wolf shall dwell with the lamb, and the leopard shall dwell with the kid…" *Isaiah 11:6 Targum*

This is simply a metaphor which means: Israel will dwell securely together with the wicked Gentiles who are symbolized as wolves and leopards. This is repeated by the prophet Jeremiah:

> "…and a wolf of the evenings shall spoil them, a leopard shall watch over their cities…"
> *Jeremiah 5:6*

All nations will return to the true faith and no longer steal or destroy. Instead, they will eat kosher food peacefully with Israel.

> "And the cow and the bear shall feed; their young ones shall lie down together: and the lion shall eat straw like the ox." *Isaiah 11:7*

There are many other Messianic prophecies like this which are metaphors. In the Messianic age everyone will understand what these metaphors and allusions really mean.

Commentary on 12.1
Rabbinical commentary for Genesis 9:3, according to John Gill, is that all the ancient rabbis said that during the Messianic age all nations would return to Noahide law and there will be no more kosher food.

12.2 Elijah and the Gog-Magog War

Our sages taught: "There will be no difference between the current age and the Messianic age except Gentile nations will no longer rule over Israel."

Ezekiel's prophecy seems to imply that the Gog-Magog war will occur at the beginning of the Messianic age. Before that war, a prophet will arise to prepare Israel's heart to seek God.

> "Behold, I will send you Elijah the prophet before the coming of the great and dreadful day of the LORD:" *Malachi 4:5*

He will not come to debate what is pure or impure, or to dispute the lineages of kings and priests. Instead, he will establish peace within the world.

> "And he shall turn the heart of the fathers to the children, and the heart of the children to their fathers, lest I come and smite the earth with a curse." *Malachi 4:6*

Some sages say that Elijah's coming will precede the coming of the Messiah. No one can know with certainty until they actually occur because neither the wise men nor the prophets give specific answers. We only have opinions on these matters. What occurs, and in what order, is not precisely stated, but they are not fundamental to the faith.

No one should spend time studying these things and similar matters because they are not essential to the faith. They will bring fear and lead you away from focusing on God's love.

Similarly, no one should try to determine the appointed time for the Messiah's coming. Our sages declared:

> "May the spirits of those who attempt to determine the time of Messiah's coming expire!"

Instead, one should just wait and not research the specifics of prophecy as we have explained.

Commentary on 12.2
The sages are trying to get us to ignore Scripture. They do not understand that the Messiah came before Titus destroyed the temple. If you want to see for yourself if this is true, they place you under a curse.

12.3 Purification of Lineage

Once the Messiah's kingdom is established and all of Israel is regathered to Him, the lineages of the entire nation will be established based on His word and the prophetic spirit which will rest upon Him.

> "And He shall sit *as* a refiner and purifier of silver: and He shall purify the sons of Levi, and purge them as gold and silver, that they may offer unto the LORD an offering in righteousness."
> *Malachi 3:3*

First, He will purify the lineage of the Levites, stating "this one is descended from a Levite priest." Those whom He does not recognize will be demoted from their positions to being simply Israelites. Ezra implies this.

> "And the Tirshatha said unto them, that they should not eat of the most holy things, till there stood up a priest with Urim and with Thummim." *Ezra 2:63*

This verse infers that the prophetic spirit is needed to discover the proper pedigree of lineage.

The Messiah will make known to each Israelite which tribe he is from, saying, "he is from this tribe and he is from that tribe." When he demotes a person from a presumed lineage, He will not state whether he is of a slave lineage or some illegitimate lineage, just that he is an Israelite from a certain tribe. This is because, according to the law, once a family has become intermingled with other Jewish tribes, they may remain intermingled.

12.4 Israel Not Under Gentile Domination

The sages and the prophets did not yearn for the Messianic age in order to have dominion over the Gentiles of the world, or to be exalted by the nations, eating, drinking, and celebrating. Instead, they desired to be free to study Torah and its wisdom without any dissention or distractions, so that they would merit the world to come.

Commentary on 12.4

The yearning to focus on God's word is good, but the sages are still mistaken by saying it gives them merit, or atonement.

12.5 No Famine or War

In that era, there will not be any famine, war, envy, or competition, because all one's needs will be abundantly supplied and all one desires will be free and plentifully available as the dust. The occupation of the entire world will be solely to know God.

The Jews will then be great sages and understand the hidden things, growing in the knowledge of their Creator according to the full extent of their human potential.

"…the earth shall be full of the knowledge of the LORD, as the waters cover the sea." *Isaiah 11:9b*

Commentary on 12.5
There will still be human sinners here during the Millennial reign. They will have a sin nature and there will be limited evil.

This ends the Law of Kings

Commentary on Noahide Law

The Importance of Noahide Law

Under the Old Covenant, a true Noahide and a true Jew will follow the laws God gave them respectively. Neither will blaspheme God; so each in his own way will accept the Messiah, meaning that true Jews and Noahides become Christians! The "Noahide Laws," as a set, are mentioned in many ancient manuscripts. The *Ancient Seder Olam 5* gives a detailed explanation of the seven Noahide laws. The *Ancient Book of Gad the Seer 9* states that those who are forbidden to convert to Judaism must remain Noahides until the coming of Messiah. The commentary on *Law of Kings 9.1* shows that the seven Noahide laws are clearly taught in Genesis 9. These are also briefly mentioned by the ancient church fathers and in the Dead Sea Scrolls. See the introduction of this book for details.

It is important to know Noahide law to understand the different Jewish religious movements. Here are the four basic groups.

- Most Christians, like Baptists, see Paul as stating the old covenant is done away with (Hebrews 8:13) and the Mosaic Law was temporary, given at mount Sinai and taken away after Christ died (Galatians 3:16-17). They have no concept of the Noahide laws, so they assume there was only the Mosaic Law and now Christ's law has replaced it. They do not consider what existed before the time of Moses.

- Traditional Judaism (Pharisees) rejects the Messiah Yeshua, but do teach the concept of the Noahide laws. Therefore, they would agree with the Christians, that Gentiles were never supposed to follow the Mosaic law.
- Messianic Judaism accepts Yeshua as the prophesied Messiah, but also believes in the Noahide Laws. Gentiles have never been bound to the Mosaic Law, but they, as a group of Jews and Gentiles, choose to adhere to the Mosaic law as part of their covenant and to be able to better witness to Jews.
- Hebrew Roots Movement is varied. Most do accept Yeshua as the Messiah, but do not know about or accept the Noahide Laws. The HRM can be loosely grouped into four sub categories:
    - Noahide Hebrew Roots are those who seek to study their Hebrew roots to understand God and prophecy better, but believe the Mosaic law was never intended for Gentiles.
    - One-Law Movement are those who reject the Noahide laws and teach that everyone must keep Sabbath, festivals, and kosher food laws, but not necessarily circumcision or animal sacrifice.
    - Two-Stick Movement are those who teach that those who observe the Sabbath, food laws, and festivals prove themselves to be the true Israel. They are either physically the ten lost tribes, but do not know it, or they are the only ones to whom the Holy Spirit is speaking on the earth in these last days. This is a kind of replacement theology.

- <u>Essene Hebrews Roots</u> are basically Noahide Hebrew Roots believers who hold that the teaching of the law and prophets should be interpreted by the Dead Sea Scrolls.

It is my conclusion that if one accepts that the Noahide laws are real and that Yeshua is the true Messiah, one would reject the doctrines of traditional Judaism, One-Law, and the Two-Stick groups. This would leave that person in either the strictly Christian camp or the Messianic / Noahide groups. Once you study the Dead Sea Scrolls and see how the Essenes taught prophecy, the minor differences between the last three groups basically disappear. A future book will be released on the history of the *School of the Prophets* as taught by the Dead Sea Scrolls for this purpose. For now, let us look at how the Pharisees twisted their own law into legalism and see examples of Noahide Law throughout the Bible.

Seven Noahide Laws

1. ABSTAIN FROM IDOLATRY
2. DO NOT COMMIT BLASPHEMY
3. DO NOT COMMIT MURDER
4. DO NOT COMMIT FORNICATION
5. DO NOT STEAL
6. DO NOT EAT BLOOD
7. ESTABLISH COURTS OF JUSTICE

Ten Commandments

1. HAVE NO OTHER GODS
2. MAKE NO GRAVEN IMAGES
3. DO NOT COMMIT BLASPHEMY
4. REMEMBER THE SABBATH DAY
5. HONOR FATHER AND MOTHER
6. DO NOT KILL
7. DO NOT COMMIT ADULTERY
8. DO NOT STEAL
9. DO NOT LIE
10. DO NOT COVET

Pharisaical Legalism

First, we want to show where the Pharisees simply took Jewish law too far by adding their traditions and making void the Word of God. When we take these out, we can clearly see Noahide law.

The basis of the legalism of the Pharisees is taking laws meant only for temple priests and applying them to everyone. When on duty, the priests are to wash their hands and instruments in a certain manner, repeat certain prayers, and do specific actions. When all of these steps were done correctly, these rituals taught prophecy. That is why it was extremely important to do them correctly. The Pharisees lost sight of the reason for these rituals and began to believe that the rituals in reality somehow made them pure.

Since each man was to be the priest in his home by leading the family in prayer and Torah study, it was not long until the Pharisees taught that if a man were truly holy he would equal or outshine the priests in the temple by his outward actions.

Entering a Gentile's Home

Pharisees reasoned that if a priest could not enter a temple of idols and a Gentile might have an idol in his home, then all Jews should be forbidden to enter the homes of Gentiles. In this case, how were they supposed to make converts? In Acts 11:3, we see Peter thinking he should not enter the home of Cornelius because he was a Gentile. What is even more amazing is the fact that Cornelius was a known God-fearer; so he would not have had an idol in his house! Why on earth would a Jew not fellowship with at Noahide who loves God and is awaiting the coming of the Messiah? God had to give Peter a dream (Acts 10:9-33) to show him that this was never meant to be. It was a perversion of the Torah.

Working on the Sabbath

Jews and Gentiles who live in the land of Israel are not to work on the Sabbath. The reason is that we all need time to rest and study the Word of God. The Pharisees thought it was a sin for Jesus' disciples to pick food to eat on the sabbath when they were hungry (Luke 6:1-5). Jesus responded to their accusation by reminding them that David was hungry and ate the priests' food (which was forbidden for non-priests). King David did this because he was serving God to the best of his ability and Saul was persecuting him for it. The disciples were likewise serving God to the best of their ability and were hungry because of it, so they ate the food they found. Again, they did not sell it, they just ate it. You will always be able to serve God better if you are not distracted by hunger or thirst.

In other examples, the Pharisees reprimanded Jesus for healing on the Sabbath (Mark 3:1-6). Jesus responded by saying the Sabbath was made for man, not man for the Sabbath (Mark 2:23-28). Could the believing woman study the word of God better if she were in pain or healed? The

Law of Moses says circumcision can be done on the Sabbath (John 7:19-23), so why not healing?

Corban

The priests are commanded to serve in the temple at certain times by course. If they are needed at home to feed their families, arrangements will be made because the temple services are most important. Again, putting regular Jews in the place of priests, the Pharisees went beyond the Law and added a new rule for Corban (giving support to the temple). According to Matthew 15:1-9, Pharisees taught that if you only have enough money feed your family (including your parents), making it impossible to tithe, you are free from the law of parental support. How evil had they become?

Touching - *Negiah*

Hugging your family members (sisters, daughters, mothers, aunts, nieces, etc.) has always been permissible. However, there is a prohibition, called *Negiah* in Hebrew, of not touching a woman in a sexual manor (hugging, petting, kissing, etc.) even if this does not lead to sexual intercourse. The rabbis extended this to not touching a woman in any way. If she is past puberty you cannot shake her hand or touch her on her sleeve. I know of a few Christian denominations who take Paul's comment that "It is good for a man not to touch a woman," found in 1 Corinthians 7:1, out of context in this same manner. We see in Matthew 19:13-15 that it was thought that children should not bother or touch a holy man like Jesus. Some of the children may have been young girls who were past puberty. This law was for their own protection; but, again, the Pharisees used it to keep them in darkness.

Conclusion

The point for this chapter is that most of the problems that the Pharisees caused were due to believing all Jews and Gentiles must strive to be as holy as the priests. They had forgotten what holiness really is.

In the following section we will concentrate on the problems the Pharisees caused for Gentile Noahides, so that we can clearly see Noahide law coexisting with Jewish law.

Noahide Law Throughout the Bible

With legalism out of the way, let us turn our attention to where we find Noahide law in the Old and New Testaments.

In the commentary for 9.1 we learned that Genesis 9 taught that Noah commanded all of his children to create their own sovereign nations with righteous courts to secure justice for all (Genesis 9:6). They all must contain laws against blasphemy, idolatry, murder, fornication, theft, and animal cruelty. They are free to add other laws that fit for their nation. When the apostle Paul said that all governments were ordained by God, in Romans 13:1-7, he was speaking about God's command through Noah about establishing Gentile courts of justice. In Romans 2:14-15, he stated that each Gentile nation has its own set of laws that will convict or excuse their behavior. These must be based on Noahide Law. We can see that the Hebrews had their own additional laws for their nation. Genesis 38:8 shows the brother-in-law law existed prior to the law of Moses. Abraham knew about the law of taking a second wife if the first one was barren (Abraham did not marry Keturah until after the deaths of both Sarah and Hagar). We see Moses teaching the Sabbath law to Israel at Elim before they arrived at Mount Sinai.

We see Noahide Law referenced in Scripture:

> "Wisdom hath builded her house, she hath hewn out her seven pillars:" *Proverbs 9:1 KJV*

Chart from 9.1
Genesis 9 is the chapter that deals with the Noahide Covenant.
Ge. 9:1, 7 Fornication is wrong because we need healthy children.
Ge. 9:3 Gentiles can eat any meat (kosher and non-kosher).
Ge. 9:4 Eating flesh from a living animal is forbidden.
Ge. 9:6 Murder is wrong; and we need courts of justice.
Ge. 9:8-9 There is only one true God, and this is His covenant.
Ge. 9:9 Gentile law is for all nations.
Ge. 9:13 The rainbow is the sign of the Noahide Covenant.
Ge. 9:16 The Noahide Covenant is a perpetual covenant.

We can clearly see that the Jews are forbidden to eat any animal that is not ritually slaughtered (kosher); but they can give it as food to a Gentile believer who lives in their land or sell it to a non-idolater. Even the righteous Gentiles eat non-kosher food.

> "Ye shall not eat of anything that dieth of itself: thou shalt give it unto the stranger [*Ger*] that is in thy gates, that he may eat it; or thou mayest sell it unto an alien [*Nochri*]:" *Deuteronomy 14:21 KJV*

Compare the epistle of James with the epistle of 1 Peter.

The epistle of James was written to "the twelve tribes scattered abroad," or to Jews (James 1:1). James reminds them to walk in the "law of liberty" (James 1:25). James previously explained this "Royal Law" (James 2:8) when he sent out the Jerusalem council's letter recorded in Acts

15. Jews remain Jews in their culture and Gentiles remain Gentiles in their own culture, all the while being brothers in Christ.

First Peter was written to the believing "strangers" (1 Peter 1:1): the *Gar* or Noahide believers. Peter explained that they were previously not even a people, but now they are "a chosen generation, a royal priesthood, an holy nation, and a peculiar people" (1 Peter 2:9-12). Gentile believers, called Christians, are priests and kings after Christ, a Melchizedekian priesthood, not an Aaronic one (Hebrews 6-9).

The Lord placed Noahide Law right beside Mosaic Law to show that the governmental law systems do not offer, nor hinder, salvation. If the rabbis would have kept this in mind, they would not have fallen into legalism and rejected the Messiah.

The New Covenant

In this chapter we want to show that there were covenants given by God to Noah and Abraham for all Gentiles, that the covenant of Moses was given to Israel alone, and that the New Covenant (New Testament of Jesus the Messiah) replaced the Mosaic covenant, so that both Jews and Gentiles may live together under one covenant.

We see in Genesis 9:9-13, the Noahide covenant was between God and all Gentiles.

The covenant between God and Abraham is found in Genesis 12, 13, 15, and 17. In this covenant God promised to create a nation out of the descendants of Abraham (Israel). They would have special laws to make them separate from the rest of the Gentiles and the Messiah would come through them.

The covenant between God and Israel was not given to the patriarchs who lived before the time of Moses.

> "The LORD made not this covenant with our fathers, but with us, *even* us, who *are* all of us here alive this day." *Deuteronomy 5:3 KJV*

The Old Covenant (Mosaic) was given only to the nation of Israel.

> "For thou *art* an holy people unto the LORD thy God: the LORD thy God hath chosen thee to be a special people unto Himself, above all people that *are* upon the face of the earth."
> *Deuteronomy 7:6 KJV*

> "He sheweth His word unto Jacob, His statutes and His judgments unto Israel. He hath not dealt so with any nation: *and as for* His judgments, they have not known them. Praise ye the LORD."
> *Psalms 147:19-20 KJV*

> "Who are Israelites; to whom *pertaineth* the adoption, and the glory, and the covenants, and the giving of the law, and the service *of God*, and the promises;" *Romans 9:4 KJV*

The New Covenant was prophesied to entirely replace, not modify, the old one.

> "Behold, the days come, saith the LORD, that I will make a new covenant with the house of Israel, and with the house of Judah: Not according to the covenant that I made with their fathers in the day *that* I took them by the hand to bring them out of the land of Egypt…" *Jeremiah 31:31-32 KJV*

The author of Hebrews quotes this verse and teaches that the Old Covenant, the law engraved on stones, was replaced.

> "For if that first *covenant* had been faultless, then should no place have been sought for the second. For finding fault with them, He saith, Behold, the days come, saith the Lord, when I will make a new covenant with the house of Israel and with the house of Judah: Not according to the covenant that I made with their fathers in the day when I took them by the hand to lead them out of the land of Egypt; because they continued not in My covenant, and I regarded them not, saith the Lord... In that He saith, A new *covenant*, He hath made the first old. Now that which decayeth and waxeth old is ready to vanish away." *Hebrews 8:7-9, 13 KJV*

> "By so much was Jesus made a surety of a better testament." *Hebrews 7:22 KJV*

> "Then said He, Lo, I come to do Thy will, O God. He taketh away the first, that He may establish the second." *Hebrews 10:9 KJV*

See also 2 Corinthians 3:7-11 and Galatians 3-4.

The Priesthood

The author of Hebrews explained that the fact that we have a New Covenant means that the priesthood and the Law had to change to accommodate it.

> "For the priesthood being changed, there is made of necessity a change also of the law. For he of

> whom these things are spoken pertaineth to another tribe, of which no man gave attendance at the altar." *Hebrews 7:12-13 KJV*

To be an Aaronic priest, one had to be a direct descendant of Levi, through Aaron. He had to retire from the priesthood at age fifty (Numbers 8:25). Jesus is our High Priest after the order of Melchizedek, not after the order of Aaron. Jesus was from the tribe of Judah, not Levi. He remains our High Priest even though He was born over 2,000 years ago. Those are just two laws about the High Priest that have changed.

Paul says not to allow anyone to judge you in the following:

> "Let no man therefore judge you in meat, or in drink, or in respect of an holyday, or of the new moon, or of the sabbath *days*: Which are a shadow of things to come; but the body *is* of Christ." *Colossians 2:16-17 KJV*

Animal Sacrifices

The author of Hebrews also makes it clear in Hebrews 10:1-18 that the law regarding animal sacrifices has changed since they all pointed to Jesus the Messiah. Currently, since there is no temple in Jerusalem, the Jews are forbidden to offer sacrifices, even if they could.

Noahides are Now Christians

Notice that true Noahides were looking for the Messiah. Once they accepted the Messiah they became Christians. Paul said there is now "neither Jew nor Gentile," but Christians (Gal 3:28-29). In Ephesians 2:14 Paul said that Jews and Gentiles are now one in Christ (in spite of the cultural differences). In Ephesians 2:19 there are no more "Gar," or Noahides, either in or outside of the land of Israel; but all believers are now "fellow saints."

Gentiles are the wild olive tree that is grafted into the Jewish olive tree, all the while remaining a wild olive branch (Romans 11:11-24). Believers were urged to continue in the grace of God (Acts 13:43), serving God in the way they were when they were saved; Jews according to their customs and Gentiles according to their customs. This is why Timothy was circumcised (Acts 16:1-3), but Titus was not (Galatians 2:3).

Real Blasphemers

The real blasphemers are those who reject the prophecies of the Messiah and reject Gentile believers. Gentile believers are those whom King David calls "those who are forgiven without the law (Rom 4:6-8)."

We have a communion table that only believers in Messiah have a right to partake of (Hebrews 13:10). David also prophesied that their "table" of ceremonial law would become a snare to the Jews.

> "Let their table become a snare before them: *and that which should have been* for *their* welfare, *let it* become a trap." *Psalms 69:22 KJV*

> "And David saith, Let their table be made a snare, and a trap, and a stumblingblock, and a recompence unto them:" *Romans 11:9 KJV*

The Jews of that day abhorred idols, but committed sacrilege by forming their own sects, replacing true Messianic Judaism (Romans 2:22). They perverted into the Karaite-Sadducee sect, the Rabbinic-Pharisee sect, and later the Gnostic-Kabbalah sect.

Circumcision

Circumcision is the very last thing an adult does when they choose to convert to Judaism. Paul made it clear that Christians are not to become circumcised. If we go through that ritual, we are saying that we convert to Judaism and accept the Law of Moses, which is the same as stating that we reject the New Covenant of Jesus the Messiah.

> "For there are many unruly and vain talkers and deceivers, specially they of the circumcision: Whose mouths must be stopped, who subvert whole houses, teaching things which they ought not, for filthy lucre's sake." *Titus 1:10-11 KJV*

> "Beware of dogs, beware of evil workers, beware of the concision. For we are the circumcision, which worship God in the spirit, and rejoice in Christ Jesus, and have no confidence in the flesh." *Philippians 3:2-3 KJV*

> "In whom also ye are circumcised with the circumcision made without hands, in putting off the body of the sins of the flesh by the circumcision of Christ:" *Colossians 2:11 KJV*

> "Stand fast therefore in the liberty wherewith Christ hath made us free, and be not entangled again with the yoke of bondage. Behold, I Paul say

> unto you, that if ye be circumcised, Christ shall profit you nothing. For I testify again to every man that is circumcised, that he is a debtor to do the whole law. Christ is become of no effect unto you, whosoever of you are justified by the law; ye are fallen from grace. For we through the Spirit wait for the hope of righteousness by faith. For in Jesus Christ neither circumcision availeth anything, nor uncircumcision; but faith which worketh by love."
> *Galatians 5:1-6 KJV*

Even those who are circumcised can't keep the Law. Why should Gentiles even try?

> "For neither they themselves who are circumcised keep the law; but desire to have you circumcised, that they may glory in your flesh."
> *Galatians 6:13 KJV*

Abraham was counted as righteous and given the promise of the blessing to all nations *before* he was circumcised, so circumcision is not part of the New Covenant.

> "For what saith the scripture? Abraham believed God, and it was counted unto him for righteousness… *Cometh* this blessedness then upon the circumcision *only*, or upon the uncircumcision also? for we say that faith was reckoned to Abraham for righteousness. How was it then reckoned? when he was in circumcision, or

> in uncircumcision? Not in circumcision, but in uncircumcision." *Romans 4:3, 9-10 KJV*

Circumcision is nothing if you twist the law by omitting Noahide law.

> "For the name of God is blasphemed among the Gentiles through you, as it is written. For circumcision verily profiteth, if thou keep the law: but if thou be a breaker of the law, thy circumcision is made uncircumcision."
> *Romans 2:24-25 KJV*

Instead we should follow the original way the Torah dictated: Jews serve God in circumcision, and Gentiles serve God the way He created them, uncircumcised.

> "But as God hath distributed to every man, as the Lord hath called everyone, so let him walk. And so ordain I in all churches. Is any man called being circumcised? let him not become uncircumcised. Is any called in uncircumcision? let him not be circumcised. Circumcision is nothing, and uncircumcision is nothing, but the keeping of the commandments of God. Let every man abide in the same calling wherein he was called."
> *1 Corinthians 7:17-20 KJV*

Food Laws

God allowed the Gentiles to eat "any living thing that moves." Later the kosher food laws were given to the Israelites.

> "Every living, moving creature will be food for you. Just as I gave you green plants before, so now you have everything." *Genesis 9:3 ISV*

When the angels and the Lord came to tell Abraham about Issacs's birth and the destruction of Sodom, Abraham served them meat with dairy and they all ate all of it. The rabbinic law of not eating meat and cheese together did not apply to them.

> "And Abraham ran out to the herd and brought a calf, tender and good. And he gave it to a young man. And he hurried to dress it. And he took butter and milk, and the calf which he had dressed, and set it before them. And he stood by them under the tree, and they ate." *Genesis 18:7-8 MKJV*

Notice that even the Gentiles (Noahides) that live in Israel alongside their Jewish neighbors could eat non-Kosher meat, and apparently, cheese with their meat.

> "You shall not eat of anything that died of itself. You may give it to the alien who is within your

gates, that he may eat it. Or you may sell it to a foreigner. For you are a holy people to Jehovah your God. You shall not boil a kid in its mother's milk." *Deuteronomy 14:21 LITV*

Jesus explained that the scribes and Pharisees were using their man-made Oral Torah to misinterpret the Law of Moses by trying to make Gentiles comply with Jewish food laws even though Deuteronomy clearly says otherwise.

"He asked them, 'Are you so ignorant? Don't you know that nothing that goes into a person from the outside can make him unclean? Because it doesn't go into his heart but into his stomach, and is expelled as waste.' (By this He declared all foods clean.)" *Mark 7:18-19 ISV*

The *Ancient Epistle of Barnabas* explains that the food laws given to the Jews are to teach typological prophecy. They are not for health reasons. Here is an excerpt on what the unclean animals represent:

"[5]Swine are animals that come when they are called only if they are hungry. If they are full, they ignore their master. They represent men who come to God when in a crisis but have no time for God when they are content. We should avoid men like this. [6]The eagle, hawk, kite, and crow are animals that don't hunt and kill their own food but steal it from other birds. They are forbidden foods because they represent laziness and coveting, resulting in sins like robbery and rape. [7]The lamprey, polypus, and cuttlefish are animals that swim at the bottom of the deep, never coming to the surface. These teach us not to consort with, nor become like, men who are ungodly, those already condemned to death. [8]The hare is an animal that multiplies rapidly and with every conception it has a different mate. They represent chambering [living together without lawful marriage], adultery, polygamy [either many wives at the same time or through divorce and remarriage], incest, and fornication in general. [9]The hyena is an animal that may look male or female depending on its age. They represent homosexuality [sodomy], bisexuality, and pedophilia. Don't even resemble such people [in cross-dressing or in mannerisms, etc.]. [10]The weasel is an animal that begins its mating ritual with its mouth [teeth]. It spiritually signifies people who rape. Avoid all such people, both men and women." *Ancient Epistle of Barnabas 10:5-10*

About the clean animals he says:

"[20]On the positive side, what did Moses mean when he said you should eat animals that have cloven hooves and chew their cud? [21]An animal that chews its cud receives food from its master and is always glad to see him, meaning we should fellowship with men who are glad to constantly study God's

> Word in order to fully understand and obey all it contains. [22]An animal that is cloven hooved represents the righteous who walks in this world but is not a part of it, because he constantly looks forward to the Rapture. [23]See how well Moses legislated. [24]Was it possible for the Jews to understand what these food laws were really for? [25]We truly understand these commandments only because the Lord has circumcised our ears and hearts with the Holy Spirit."
> *Ancient Epistle of Barnabas 10:20-25*

I think the apostle Paul made it clear by saying:

> "Let no man therefore judge you in meat, or in drink, or in respect of an holyday, or of the new moon, or of the sabbath *days*: Which are a shadow of things to come; but the body is of Christ."
> *Colossians 2:16-17 KJV*

Sabbath

God created the weekly Sabbath as a sign of the covenant between Him and the children of Israel.

> "Speak thou also unto the children of Israel, saying, Verily My sabbaths ye shall keep: for it *is* a sign between Me and you throughout your generations; that *ye* may know that I *am* the LORD that doth sanctify you. Ye shall keep the sabbath therefore; for it *is* holy unto you: everyone that defileth it shall surely be put to death: for whosoever doeth *any* work therein, that soul shall be cut off from among his people. Six days may work be done; but in the seventh *is* the sabbath of rest, holy to the LORD: whosoever doeth *any* work in the sabbath day, he shall surely be put to death. Wherefore the children of Israel shall keep the sabbath, to observe the sabbath throughout their generations, *for* a perpetual covenant. **It *is* a sign between Me and the children of Israel for ever**: for *in* six days the LORD made heaven and earth, and on the seventh day He rested, and was refreshed."
> *Exodus 31:13-17 KJV*

This same idea is reiterated in Ezekiel 20:12.

> "Moreover also I gave them My sabbaths, to be a sign between Me and them, that they might know that I *am* the LORD that sanctify them."
> *Ezekiel 20:12 KJV*

The Essenes (keepers of the Dead Sea Scrolls) held this same view that the Sabbath was a sign between God and the nation of Israel alone.

> "And the Creator of all things blessed it, but **He did not sanctify all peoples and nations to keep Sabbath thereon, but Israel alone**: them alone He permitted to eat and drink and to keep Sabbath thereon on the earth."
> *Ancient Book of Jubilees 2:31*

The Holy Spirit more fully explained in Deuteronomy that His covenant with Israel was different than the covenant He made with their fathers.

> "And Moses called all Israel, and said unto them, Hear, O Israel, the statutes and judgments which I speak in your ears this day, that ye may learn them, and keep, and do them. The LORD our God made a covenant with us in Horeb. **The LORD made not this covenant with our fathers**, but with us, *even* us, who *are* all of us here alive this day."
> *Deuteronomy 5:1-3 KJV*

The Israelites were to be careful and allow the Gentiles who lived in their nation to also have off one day in seven.

> "But the seventh day *is* the sabbath of the LORD thy God: *in it* thou shalt not do any work, thou, nor thy son, nor thy daughter, nor thy manservant, nor thy maidservant, nor thine ox, nor thine ass, nor any of thy cattle, nor **thy stranger that *is* within thy gates**; that thy manservant and thy maidservant may rest as well as thou." *Deuteronomy 5:14*

Paul states that there were Jewish believers who continued to keep the Sabbath and Gentile believers who did not. He did not want one group to judge the other; but he also did not want anyone to violate their conscience. So, he taught the believers:

> "One man esteemeth one day above another: another esteemeth every day *alike*. Let every man be fully persuaded in his own mind." *Romans 14:5*

Didn't the disciples meet on the sabbath to worship? No. On the Sabbath they went into the synagogues of the Jews to witness to unbelievers. We see this in Acts 13:5, 14-16, 42-48; 14:1; 17:1-4, 10-12, 16-17; 18:4-7, 19; 19:8-9.

Their pattern for Christian worship was to meet on the first day of the week, Sunday morning.

> "And upon the first *day* of the week, when the disciples came together to break bread, Paul preached unto them, ready to depart on the morrow; and continued his speech until midnight."
> *Acts 20:7 KJV*

Paul even instructed them to bring offerings on Sunday when they came to church. If they worshipped on the Sabbath, Paul would have instructed them to bring offerings then.

> "Upon the first *day* of the week let every one of you lay by him in store, as *God* hath prospered him, that there be no gatherings when I come."
> *1 Corinthians 16:2 KJV*

Questions

"Isn't the New Testament (the new covenant) just a correction of the Old Testament (old covenant)?"

No, Paul says the new covenant has completely replaced the old covenant.

> "In that He says, 'A NEW COVENANT,' He has made the first obsolete. Now what is becoming obsolete and growing old is ready to vanish away."
> *Hebrews 8:13 NKJV*

"That would mean the Law of God, the Torah, is obsolete. That can't be right."

It is not the "Law of God" we are talking about. It is the temporary Law of Sinai that God gave the Israeli nation for a set time. Aaronic priests must come from the line of Aaron and retire by the age of fifty. Jesus would not have qualified to be our high priest, nor could He have continued past the age of fifty if He were of the Aaronic priesthood. Jesus was ordained a Melchizedekian priest. That means the Law had to change with it as well.

"For the priesthood being changed, of necessity there is also a change of the law."
Hebrews 7:12 NKJV

"Didn't Jesus say He did not come to abolish the Law but fulfill it, and that none of it would pass away until everything is fulfilled?"

"Do not think that I have come to destroy the Law or the Prophets. I have not come to destroy but to fulfill. For truly I say to you, Till the heaven and the earth pass away, not one jot or one tittle shall in any way pass from the Law **until all is fulfilled**."
Matthew 5:17-18 MKJV

Yes, and the apostle John stated, "all was fulfilled" when Jesus died on the cross.

"After this, knowing that **all things were now accomplished**, that the Scripture might be fulfilled, Jesus said, I thirst. Then a vessel full of vinegar was set. And they filled a sponge with sour wine and put it upon hyssop, and put it to His mouth. Then when Jesus had received the sour wine, He said, **It is finished!** And He bowed His head and gave up the spirit." *John 19:28-30 MKJV*

John the Baptist was the last prophet / priest of the age of the Aaronic priesthood and its temporary law.

> "For all the Prophets and the Law prophesied until John." *Matthew 11:13 MKJV*

"Couldn't I, as a Gentile believer, do the ritual of the Nazarite vow of Numbers 6?"

No. We see in a discussion between Paul and James that Paul was accused of teaching that both Jews and Gentiles outside of the land of Israel should avoid the Law of Moses (circumcision, food laws, sabbaths, etc.).

> "but they [the Jews] have been informed about you that you teach all the Jews who are among the Gentiles to forsake Moses, saying that they ought not to circumcise *their* children nor to walk according to the customs." *Acts 21:21 NKJV*

To smooth things over, James asked Paul to join four Jews in publicly performing the Nazarite vow. Paul was to pay for himself and the others to show he believed that Jews should still follow the Mosaic law.

> "What then? The assembly must certainly meet, for they will hear that you have come. Therefore, do what we tell you: We have four men who have

> taken a vow. Take them and be purified with them, and pay their expenses so that they may shave *their* heads, and that all may know that those things of which they were informed concerning you are nothing, but *that* you yourself also walk orderly and keep the law." *Acts 21:22-24 NKJV*

Notice what James says after that. James said he would remind the Jews of the letter he sent to the Gentiles in Acts 15. The letter stated that Gentiles did not have to follow the Mosaic Law. Here James went further, stating that Gentiles are *forbidden* to follow Jewish law (the rituals).

> "But concerning the Gentiles who believe, we have written *and* decided that **they should observe no such thing**, except that they should keep themselves from *things* offered to idols, from blood, from things strangled, and from sexual immorality." *Acts 21:25 NKJV*

The letter they sent out said the same thing.

> "Because we have heard that certain ones who went out from us have troubled you with words, unsettling your souls, saying, **Be circumcised and keep the law**! (to whom **we gave no such command**);" *Acts 15:24 MKJV*

Are there any other references in the Mishna that could point to the idea that the Law of Moses held Jews to a different standard than it did Gentiles?

Yes. The Mishna and Talmud are full of examples. Here are just a few:

- Gentiles cannot create *tefillin* (the object Jews place on their heads and hands for prayer) or *Mezuzah* (the object Jews place on their doorposts). (tefillin, Mezuzah 1.11, 13)

- Gentiles may not create *Tzitzit* (prayer shawls). (Tzitzit 1.12) Numbers 15:38 suggests that only the children of Israel can create Tzitzit.

- A circumcised Gentile who wishes to convert must still go through the ritual of "extracting the blood of the covenant" on the day that he converts. (Milah 1.7)

- A Gentile may work for himself on the Sabbath, but he cannot work for Jews on the Sabbath. (Shabbat 2.10, 6.1)

- A Jew can sell leaven to Gentiles before Passover starts since Gentiles do not practice Passover rituals. (Chametz U'Matzah 5.9)

- A Gentile is not to build a sukkah for Sukkot observance. (Chametz U'Matzah 5.9)

- Gentiles and resident aliens (Noahides) do not tithe the half-shekel Temple tax. (Shekalim 4.8)
- Gentiles are not obligated to kindle the Hanukkah candles. (Megillah vChanukah 3.2)

- *Kiddushin* (marriage contracts) are never given to Gentile brides. (Ishut 4.15)

- The prohibition of sexual intercourse with a woman when she is menstruating or in the forty days after giving birth does not apply to Gentiles. (Issurei Biah 4.4)

- Gentiles are not required to circumcise or immerse (mikvah). (Issurei Biah 14.7)

- The only sexual relations forbidden to a Gentile are: his mother, his father's wife, his maternal sister, a married woman, a male, and an animal. (Issurei Biah 14.10) Other relations forbidden the Jews are permitted to them if it is legal in their country. (Issurei Biah 14.26)

- Gentiles are allowed to castrate their animals; Jews are not. (Issurei Biah 16.13)

- Gentiles cannot be Nazarites (Nezirut 2.16)

- Peace-offerings, meal-offerings, sin-offerings, or guilt-offerings are not accepted from a Gentile. (Maaseh Hakorbanot 3.2)

- Gentiles are permitted to offer burnt offerings to God in all places, provided they sacrifice them on a raised structure that they build. It is forbidden to help them, for Jews are forbidden to sacrifice outside of the temple courtyard. Jews are permitted to instruct Gentiles and teach them how to sacrifice to the Almighty. (Maaseh Hakorbanot 19.16)

- The prohibitions of *piggul*[b], *notar*[c], or sacrificial meat that has become impure do not apply with regard to sacrifices brought by Gentiles.[d] (Pesulei Hamukdashim 18.24)

- Gentiles do not become unclean from a *beit Hapras* (plowing over grave in a field) like Jews do. (Tum'at Met 9.6)

- A Jewish man with a seminal discharge becomes ritualistically impure, but a Gentile with a seminal discharge does not become impure. (She'ar Avot haTum'ah 5.16- 17)

---

[b] Sacrificial meat not eaten according to ritual.

[c] Sacrificial meat not eaten within the allotted time after the ritual.

[d] Jews must destroy any offering in this state while Gentiles do not have to throw out the food.

Isn't the Law of Moses (Exodus through Deuteronomy) God's commandments to individuals? And therefore, wouldn't it still be binding on every person on earth?

Actually, no. Look closely at this outline and you can see that God was instructing Moses to set up a legal court system, as Noah had commanded, for the government of the nation of Israel to properly punish those who violated their laws. Therefore, it was binding on everyone living in Israel during the time that law / court system was enforced.

Exodus

1-6 History of Moses and Israel

7-11 History of the Plagues of Egypt

12 History of Passover night in Egypt (temporary blood on doorposts); Gentiles (nochri) forbidden to observe Passover. Only the circumcised are allowed to keep Passover (vv. 43-44)

13 Temporary consecration of firstborn (v. 1),

13 Israeli observance of Festival of Unleavened Bread (vv. 2-16), when in the promised land (v. 5)

13 Pillars of Cloud and Fire (vv. 17-22)

14-17 Crossing the Red Sea to Mount Sinai

18 Israeli supreme court set up (Noahide-like courts recommended by Jethro)

20 10 Commandments (v. 10) (how they were to enforce them) (v. 10 Gentile residents also allowed to rest on Sabbath)

20 Laws about temporary altars (v. 22-26)

21 How judges are to rule, v. 1
On enslavement / incarceration (vv. 1-32)
Restitution (21:33-22:15)

22 Punishments for murder, stealing, etc. (22:16-23:9)

23 Land Sabbath, Sabbath and festivals (vv. 10-19), boiling a kid in its mother's milk (v. 19)

24 Covenant confirmed with Moses, Aaron and his sons, and the seventy elders (the government of Israel)
25-30 Construction of the tabernacle, ark, table of bread, menorah, priest clothes, etc.
31 Sabbath (vv. 12-18) (v. 17 It is a sign between God and the children of Israel forever.)
32-40 History
35 Prohibition of kindling a fire on the Sabbath (v. 3)

Leviticus

1-4 Priestly offerings for Israelis
(1) Burnt offerings (before temple, v. 5 they cannot complete the ritual without priests) (2) Grains offerings (3) Peace offerings (4) Sin (trespass) offerings
5-7 Court rulings of various sins, if there is a witness (5:1)
8-9 Aaron and sons consecrated
10 Nadab and Abihu offer strange fire and are killed
11 Kosher food laws for Israelis
12 Purification after childbirth (women only)
13-14 Priestly inspections for leprosy
15 Bodily discharges
16 Day of Atonement
17 Place of sacrifice (vv. 1-9)
17 Punishment for eating of blood (vv. 10-16)
18 Punishment for unlawful sexual relations (v. 29)
19 No sacrifices eaten after 3rd day (vv. 1-8)
19 Various regulations and punishments for honoring parents, leftover sacrifices, gleaning fields, etc. (vv. 9-37)
20 Punishments (child sacrifice vv. 1-9), (immorality vv. 10-21), (other vv. 22-27)
21-22 Holiness and the priests (22:2)
22 How priests are to accept offerings and sacrifices from different people groups (vv. 17-33)
23 Regulations on the feasts of the Lord (Sabbath and festivals)
24 Lamps (vv. 1-4), bread for the tabernacle (vv. 5-9), punishment for blasphemy (vv. 10-16), an eye for an eye (vv. 17-23)
25 Shemitah and Jubilee regulations

27 Laws about vows

Numbers

3-4 Laws governing the Levites

5 Priestly rituals: inspection of the leper (vv. 1-4), trespass offering (vv. 5-10), water of bitterness (vv. 11-31)

6 Nazarite vows (vv. 1-21), Aaronic blessing (vv. 22-27)

8 Cleansing of the Levites (vv. 5-22), retirement of the Levites (vv. 23-26)

9 Passover (vv. 1-14) Gentiles (ger) are allowed to keep Passover if they choose to, but must be circumcised (v. 14).

10 Creation and use of the silver Trumpets by the priests (vv. 1-10)

15 Laws about sacrifices (v. 15 some Gentile sacrifices are allowed), laws about unintentional sins (vv. 22-31), priests (v. 25), tassels on garments (vv. 37-41)

18 Duties of priests and Levites

19 Priestly ritual of the red heifer

28-29 Offerings (priests) (daily, vv. 1-8)

30 Regulations on vows

35 Cities of Levites (vv. 1-8), cites of refuge (vv. 9-34)

Deuteronomy

4 Punishments of idolatry (vv. 15-40), cities of refuge (vv. 41-43)

5 Ten Commandments (vv. 14-15 Gentiles allowed to rest on Sabbath)

6 Law about the *tefillin* and *mezuzah* (vv. 6-9)

7 Command to destroy all idolatry in the land of Israel

10 True circumcision of the heart (vv. 12-22)

11 Regulations governing the *tefillin* and *mezuzah* (vv. 18-20)

12 Law stating sacrifices are to only be in Jerusalem (v. 13) replaces the law of temporary altars (Exodus 20:22-26)

14 Kosher laws and temple tithes

15 Sabbath (Shemitah) year regulations

16 Laws for Passover, Shavuot, Sukkot, courts, and Asherah trees

18 Punishments for occult practices (vv. 9-14), prophecy of the messianic prophet (vv. 15-22)

19 Regulations for cities of refuge (vv. 1-13), landmarks and witnesses (vv. 14-21)

20 Laws of wartime in Israel

21 Atonement for unsolved murders (vv. 1-9), marrying female captives (vv. 10-14), inheritance rights of the firstborn (vv. 15-17), punishment for a rebellious son (vv. 18-21), man hung on a tree is cursed (vv. 22-23)

22 Various regulations (vv. 1-12), punishment for sexual immorality (vv. 13-30)

23 Laws of excommunication (vv. 1-8), various other laws (vv. 15-25)

24 Laws about proper divorce papers (vv. 1-4), various laws (24:5-25:4)

25 Special laws of Levite marriage (vv. 5-10), various laws (vv. 11-19)

26 Offerings of firstfruits and tithes

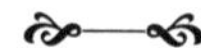

Appendices

Idolatry

As explained in *Law of Kings 9.2,* idolatry is the same from the standpoint of the Mosaic law and the Noahide law. Therefore, it should be viewed the same from a Christian perspective as well. The tractate in the Mishna that explains what is and is not idolatry is called the *Avodah Zarah*, which means "foreign worship." Parts of it are quoted here so we can gain a complete understanding of idolatry. It is divided into four sections.

Section 1 describes avoiding doing business with pagans when they are celebrating a festival to a pagan god. If the festival is secular, it does not have to be avoided. Saturnalia and Kalends are given as examples of holidays that were not pagan in origin but became pagan over time. If Gentiles have decorations or statues of their kings, they are only avoided if they are used in worship. Worship is defined as bowing down in front of an idol and praying to the god it represents. One is forbidden to make idols, idol paraphernalia, jewelry, or other ornaments used in idolatrous worship. One should not possess or wear occult jewelry, for instance. One should not rent to anyone who might bring an idol into your apartment or home.

Section 2 describes why we are not to help, sell to, or buy from anyone who is starting a pilgrimage to go worship an idol.

Section 3 states that if a Jew finds an idol, he must grind it to powder to completely destroy it. Whatever is held as sacred or treated with respect is part of idolatry. Whatever is treated as a common thing is not part of idolatry. If there is an idol in a public place, like a bathhouse or restaurant, one need not avoid it. If the building is a shrine to a god or goddess, it must be avoided. If pagans worship the hills, mountains or trees as divine but do not alter them in any way, they are not to be destroyed, because they are God's creation. It then asks the question,

> "Why are Asherah trees forbidden? Because idolaters planted them for the purpose of idolatry. Any idolatrous thing that human hands created is forbidden."

Later the question is asked,

> "What is an Asherah tree? Every tree that has an idol under it."

Idolatry is described this way. If an idol is simply placed in a house, on a pillar, or under a tree, then the idol should be removed and destroyed, but the house, pillar, or tree should be left alone. If a shrine (house), pillar, or tree was created for the purpose of idolatry, it must be destroyed along with the idol. If a house, pillar, or tree was modified to house an idol, then the idol must be destroyed, and the house or pillar must be put back to the way it was before the modification was done to it. If a tree was made into an Asherah tree by creating a place under it to house the idol, then after destroying the idol, it may be trimmed to desecrate the idol, or it can simply be left alone to grow back to its original state. It is then no longer an Asherah tree.

Section 4 teaches about *nullification.* To nullify an idol, a Jew must grind the idol to powder and cast it to the wind. He can derive no benefit from it. A Gentile may simply deface the idol (e.g. cut off its nose). He then may melt it down and use or sell the scrap metal. He cannot sell it as it is if someone may fix it and use it as an idol again.

> "If he cut off the tip of its ear, the tip of its nose, the tip of a finger, or if he dented it even though he did not diminish it, he has nullified it."

Nullification is different for a Jew than for a Gentile in other ways as well.

> "A Gentile can nullify any idol, but a Jew cannot nullify the idol of a Gentile. When a Gentile nullifies an idol, its paraphernalia are also nullified. But if the paraphernalia are nullified, the idol still needs to be nullified."

Idolatry and the Trinity

Some modern Jews will look at Christians as idol worshipers because we worship Jesus the Messiah as God incarnate. It can easily be demonstrated from the patriarchal writings of the Dead Sea Scrolls, the *Book of*

Gad the Seer, and the fragments of the *Book of Nathan the Prophet* that many current and ancient Jews worshiped the one true God in His triune form. The apostle Paul confirmed this ancient Essene view of God when he wrote that from the beginning of creation everyone who knew God knew of His godhead. The Pharisees who rejected the writings of the patriarchs are without excuse.

> "For the invisible things of Him from the creation of the world are clearly seen, being understood by the things that are made, *even* His eternal power and Godhead; so that they are without excuse:"
> *Romans 1:20 KJV*

Definitions

Acum (ah-koom): idolater

B'nai Noah (beh-**nai**): children of Noah

B'nai Israel (beh-**nai**): children of Israel

Ben nechar (ben nay-**khar)**: identical with a nochri

Ezrach (ez-**rakh)**: native born Jew

Ger Toshav (gār tō-**shav)**: Noahide living in Israel

Ger b'Shaarecha (gār bi-shah-**reh**-kha): Noahide living among Jews

Ger Tzedek (gār tseh-**dek)**: a convert

Gerim (gār-**eem)**: Jewish coverts or righteous Noahides

Gioret (gār-**et)**: female convert or Noahide

Hasid (ha-sid): pious Jew

Hasidei Umot HaOlam (ha-si-**dā** oo-**mōt** ha-ō-**lahm**): a pious Gentile

Messianic Age: Age of final redemption

Nochri (nōk-**ree)**: a Gentile who refuses to obey the Seven Noahide Laws

Noahide: a Gentile who observes the seven Noahide Laws

Noahide Ger (gār): a Gentile who observes the seven Noahide Laws

Yeshiva (yeh-**shee**-vah): a Torah School

Zar (zahr): (stranger), a Jew who is not a Cohen.

Other Books by Ken Johnson, Th.D.

- **Ancient Post-Flood History,** Historical Documents That Point to a Biblical Creation.
- **Ancient Seder Olam,** A Christian Translation of the 2000-year-old Scroll
- **Ancient Prophecies Revealed,** 500 Prophecies Listed in Order of When They Were Fulfilled
- **Ancient Book of Jasher,** Referenced in Joshua 10:13; 2 Samuel 1:18; 2 Timothy 3:8
- **Third Corinthians,** Ancient Gnostics and the End of the World
- **Ancient Paganism,** The Sorcery of the Fallen Angels
- **The Rapture,** The Pretribulational Rapture of the Church Viewed from the Bible and the Ancient Church
- **Ancient Epistle of Barnabas,** His Life and Teaching
- **The Ancient Church Fathers,** What the Disciples of the Apostles Taught
- **Ancient Book of Daniel**
- **Ancient Epistles of John and Jude**
- **Ancient Messianic Festivals,** And the Prophecies They Reveal
- **Ancient Word of God**
- **Cults and the Trinity**
- **Ancient Book of Enoch**
- **Ancient Epistles of Timothy and Titus**

- **Fallen Angels**
- **Ancient Book of Jubilees**
- **The Gnostic Origins of Calvinism**
- **The Gnostic Origins of Roman Catholicism**
- **Demonic Gospels**
- **The Pre-Flood Origins of Astrology**
- **The End-Times by the Church Fathers**
- **Ancient Book of Gad the Seer**
- **Ancient Apocalypse of Ezra**, called 2 Esdras in the KJV
- **Ancient Testaments of the Patriarchs,** Autobiographies from the Dead Sea Scrolls

- **DVD 1 – The Prophetic Timeline**
- **DVD 2 – The Church Age**

For more information, visit us at:

Biblefacts.org

Bibliography

Johnson, Ken, *Ancient Epistle of Barnabas*, Createspace, 2010

Clorfene, Chiam, *The World of the Ger*, Createspace, 2014

Clorfene, Chiam, *The Path of the Righteous Gentile*, Targum Press, 1987

Eerdmans Publishing, *Ante-Nicene Fathers*, Eerdmans Publishing, 1886

Bercot, David, *A Dictionary of Early Christian Beliefs*, Hendrickson Publishers, 1999

Whiston, William, *The Works of Flavius Josephus*, London, Miller & Sowerby, 1987. Includes Antiquities of the Jews.

Cruse, C. F., *Eusebius' Ecclesiastical History*, Hendrickson Publishers, 1998

Made in the USA
Middletown, DE
06 October 2018